2-

THE NOT-YE

On The Hudson

Jung

BOOK SERIES

The New York Center for Jungian Studies presents conferences and seminars in the U.S. and abroad, including its Jung On The Hudson seminars held each summer in the historic Hudson Valley. The N.Y. Center seminars, book series and continuing education programs are designed for individuals from all fields as well as mental health professionals who are interested in exploring the relevance of Jung's ideas to their personal lives and/or professional activities. The Center offers individual, couple and group counseling, and provides consulting services and mediation for family businesses and corporations.

For more information, please contact:
The New York Center for Jungian Studies
121 Madison Avenue, New York, NY 10016
Telephone: 212-689-8238 or Fax: 212-889-7634

the NOT-YET-TRANSFORMED GOD

GOD

DEPTH PSYCHOLOGY AND THE INDIVIDUAL RELIGIOUS EXPERIENCE

JANET O. DALLETT

NICOLAS-HAYS, INC.
York Beach, Maine

First published in 1998 by
NICOLAS-HAYS, INC.
P. O. Box 2039
York Beach, ME 03910-2039
Distributed to the trade by
Samuel Weiser, Inc.
Box 612
York Beach, ME 03910-0612

Library of Congress Cataloging-in-Publication Data

Dallett, Janet .
    The not-yet-transformed God : depth psychology and
the individual religious experience / Janet O. Dallett.
        p.   cm.
    "A Jung on the Hudson book"--T.p. verso
    Includes bibliographical references and index.
    ISBN 0-89254-042-7 (alk. paper)
    1. Psychoanalysis and religion.   2. Jungian psychology.
3. Jung, C. G. (Carl Gustav), 1875-1961--Religion.
I. Title
BF175.4.R44D35   1998
150.19'54--dc21   98-21648
                                                        CIP

MG
Cover and text design by Kathryn Sky-Peck
Cover art is Gauguin's "Vision after the Sermon."
Used by permission of the National Gallery of Scotland.
Typeset in 11 point Centaur
Printed in the United States of America
05 04 03 02 01 00 99 98
10 9 8 7 6 5 4 3 2 1

"All the gods are coming down from the sky and the mountaintops into the cities and towns, pouring into the world. It is terrifying."
—DREAM OF A PATIENT IN ANALYSIS

The art on the cover—Gauguin's "The Vision after the Sermon: Jacob Wrestling with the Angel"—shows Breton women witnessing a Biblical event as literal reality. Gauguin's 1888 painting speaks to our inner experience whenever the numinous breaks into everyday life and we have to wrestle psychologically to transform it.

CONTENTS

To David

PREFACE

The kind of writing I do confronts me with a painful dilemma: my profession as a psychotherapist requires me not to talk about my patients, while my vocation as a writer demands that I speak openly about some of the things that happen in the consulting room. The conflict is a little like being in love with two men at the same time, or worshipping two gods that are at war with one another.

In this book as in others, my imperfect solution is to disguise patients who do not want to be identified, changing their names and superficial facets of their outer lives, but holding scrupulously to the truth as I see it with regard to the inner events that are the point of my writing. Similarly, I sometimes cloak colleagues, relatives, friends, and enemies in protective coloring to avoid the wrath I feel I would bring upon myself if I named them. I do not write to expose individuals, but to make the reality of the psyche visible, for until the hidden corners of human psychology are seen *in vivo*, words like "psyche," "Self," and "archetype" remain abstract and unreal.

In the past, I also changed some names capriciously, believing that random obfuscation would make it harder for anyone bent on tracking down the outer-world reality of the people whose identities it is important to conceal. I have come to see this as problematical, however, and in the present book have only camouflaged people I fear might try to harm me if they were named, and those I believe would themselves be hurt by exposure, primarily my patients.

In earlier work I gave the pseudonym Sean to my second husband, the companion of my mature years. Recently I began to feel trapped by that fiction, for the further I venture into the depths of the psyche the more important I feel it is to ground myself and others in simple, everyday outer-world facts. In this book I have called my husband David by his real name. "Sean" in earlier publications is the same person as David here and in my life.

• • •

I am grateful to all the patients with whom I have worked over the years, especially those who have allowed me to write about their struggles; and to the analysts who, for better or worse, have accompanied me on my path. Ultimately, my patients and my analysts are the people from whom I have learned the most about the psyche.

Warm thanks go to the members of my writers' group, some of whom have been working together for nearly fourteen years. My writing and my life would both be poorer without the keen critical faculties, honesty, and friendship of Alex Fowler, Marge Koch-Critchfield, Carolyn Latteier, David Mathieson, and Jacqueline Rickard.

I appreciate the candid and perceptive comments about Tamanawas, an experiment in alternative care for psychotic episodes, written by Nick Dallett, Gerry Gahagan, Sarah Light, Stacy Sabella, and two people who want to remain anonymous. Portions of their accounts are included in chapter 2.

I owe a particular debt of gratitude to three people who came into my life in somewhat fateful ways and became powerful allies before I even knew them. Without them, this book could not have been completed.

Long before I had ever heard of Eugene Monick, he helped bring about the publication of my first book. After reading one of my articles, Gene mentioned me to Daryl Sharp at Inner City Books, who contacted me and eventually decided to publish *When the Spirits Come Back*. By the time Daryl asked to see it, nearly one hundred publishers had turned it down, and I was about to give up. Several years later, Gene chaired a committee that invited me to present a lecture at the 1991 National Conference of Jungian Analysts held in Minneapolis, MN. A revised version of that lecture became the seminal chapter of the present book.

Jean Matlack was chairperson of the committee that invited me to speak at the 1992 Friends' Conference on Religion and Psychology in Annville, PA. Three chapters of this book were first written as lectures for the conference, and Jean later took on the task of duplicating and distributing them to interested readers.

After failing in my first attempts to turn the lectures into a book, I put the project aside and fell into the doldrums. In 1996 I took up the material again, inspired by a letter of appreciation for my writing. The letter was from Robin Robertson, who subsequently asked to read the manuscript and made invaluable editorial suggestions. His enthusiasm, support, and substantial assistance provided the energy and direction I needed to finish the book.

chapter one

TO BEGIN

Vocatus atque non vocatus deus aderit.
(Invoked or not invoked the god will be present.)
—THE ORACLE AT DELPHI[1]

Hilde Kirsch, the woman who, together with her husband James, first brought the work of C. G. Jung to Los Angeles, told me near the end of her life that she was only just beginning to understand what she was doing in her work with patients. I was incredulous. Although I had not yet finished my training as a Jungian analyst, I was quite full of myself and believed that I knew exactly what I was doing. Thirty years later I understand what Hilde was talking about, for I become increasingly aware of how difficult it is to grasp the complexities of Jung's vision. Although his ideas have become quite popular, if controversial, Jung's followers and detractors alike tend

---

[1] This inscription is carved over the door of C. G. Jung's house.

to pass over the subtleties, which results in serious misapplications and distortions of his meaning. For my part, after studying Jung's writings for forty years, I feel that I am barely beginning to fathom the implications of his observations, particularly about the religious aspects of the psyche.

In "Psychotherapists or the Clergy,"[2] Jung wrote that every patient over the age of 35 who had come to him for help during the preceding thirty years was suffering from a religious problem. He did not mean that people should go to church, even though he was careful not to interfere with the adaptation of patients whose needs were met by conventional religion. He was referring to the fact that everyone has to come to terms with the energy and images of divinity that manifest in the human psyche, even people who do not believe in God or think of themselves as religious. The pervasive presence of such energies has practical, down-to-earth repercussions in all areas of life. When we do not find constructive solutions to the problem of God, it finds its own unconscious solutions, often the destructive ones of neurosis, psychosis, physical illness, and various problems of interpersonal power, of submission and domination, that are created when we project divine and demonic images on ordinary human beings.

Whether or not a person is conscious of the images and energies of divinity, there seems to be a fundamental human tendency to believe in and even sacrifice oneself to something larger than the small personal life. We need to feel that our lives are meaningful and valuable when set against an implacable inner criterion that says, "This is what you were born to be, and you must strive to fulfill it."

The search for meaning and value in life requires the individual to pay careful attention to inner and outer events that feel important, to

---

[2] CW 11, ¶509. CW in the footnotes refers to *The Collected Works of C. G. Jung* (Bollingen Series XX), 20 vols., trans. R. F. C. Hull, eds. H. Read, M. Fordham, G. Adler, W. McGuire (Princeton: Princeton University Press, 1953–1979). Specific citations are to the numbered paragraphs in these volumes.

honor the sense of significance even in the most loathsome or apparently trivial places. This is religion in the most basic sense of the word. As Jung puts it:

> Religion appears to me to be a peculiar attitude of mind which could be formulated in accordance with the original use of the word *religio*, which means a careful consideration and observation of certain dynamic factors that are conceived as "powers": spirits, daemons, gods, laws, ideas, ideals, or whatever name man has given to such factors in his world as he has found powerful, dangerous, or helpful enough to be taken into careful consideration, or grand, beautiful, and meaningful enough to be devoutly worshipped and loved.[3]

The religious part of the psyche is at work whenever you pay attention to something that is numinous to you, whether or not other people feel it is important. "Archetype" is Jung's word for the psychological image of a god, and when an archetype is activated, we speak of its impact as numinous. In other words, numinosity is the charge of energy in whatever we experience as divine or demonic. If you want to know what is numinous to you, consider what you find fascinating, compelling, thrilling, mysterious, horrifying, gripping, tremendous, terrifying, dreadful, or awesome. Think about the things with which you are preoccupied in spite of yourself.

Numen, the Latin word from which "numinous" is derived, refers to the living spirit once believed to inhabit everything, even inanimate matter. It means "to nod," a hint that when attention is paid to something numinous, there is a response from the other side. In a manner of speaking, the god in the icon nods.

---

[3] CW 11, ¶8.

For me, hearing about the January 1994 earthquake in Los Angeles was a numinous experience. It was as if a giant hand reached down and committed a random act of violence to the place I once called home. My emotions and imagination were struck, as though by lightning, and I was filled with terror and awe. By the same token, for many people all over the world, the 1997 death of Diana Spencer, the former Princess of Wales, was a highly-charged religious experience.

Numinosity is not only present in large, public events. Anyone who pays attention to the psyche's religious impulses is likely to discover divine energy in the small occurrences of daily life. For example, one day I was standing in front of the bread counter in the corner grocery store, perusing my shopping list, when I heard something fall on the floor near my feet. Without thinking about it, I bent down and picked it up. It was a set of keys. I handed it to its owner, a woman of about my age standing next to me. Our eyes met, she thanked me, and I realized that she was someone whose path has crossed mine a number of times over the years. On this occasion she looked extremely depressed.

On the face of it, the brief contact was trivial; it felt intense and weighty to me, however, and it stuck in my mind. The incident had the quality of a dream image and I found myself ruminating on its symbolism, imagining that the woman had lost the keys to her life, and wondering if I could help her find them.

A few days later she called me and asked for an appointment. On the level of ordinary reality I was surprised, but a part of me that lives in a less rational realm almost *expected* to hear from her. The incident in the grocery store had been numinous to me and appeared to have touched a similar place in her. The fact that she took it seriously enough to call me suggested a fundamentally religious outlook that I felt augured well for her capacity to work analytically. Therefore I accepted her as a patient without the usual preliminary interview. The validity of such an assessment always needs to be verified, and this one proved to be correct. The stuck place in my new patient's psyche soon began to move, and her depression lifted after only a few sessions.

• • •

For centuries, the traditional religions have provided countless numbers of people with more or less constructive solutions to the problem of God. Today, however, many individuals cannot accept dogmatic answers to their religious problems. For them, the church or temple is no longer an adequate vessel for God. Many, perhaps the majority, do not even believe that God exists. It is a dangerous time, for the enormous energies that have long been attached to images of divinity are now wandering Earth, as it were, looking for places to live. Raw, uncontained God-energy is pure nature, and as the ancient alchemist Dorn observed, "There is nothing in nature that does not contain as much evil as good."[4] The Judeo-Christian tradition has given the name of Satan, or the devil, to this paradoxical natural energy. Others have called it Mercurius. A German fairytale, "The Spirit in the Bottle," tells of the perils and rewards that await anyone who sets the spirit free:

> Once upon a time there was a poor woodcutter. He had an only son, whom he wished to send to [the university]. However, since he could give him only a little money to take with him, it was used up long before [graduation]. So the son went home and helped his father with the work in the forest. Once, during the midday rest, he roamed the woods and came to an immense old oak. There he heard a voice calling from the ground, "Let me

---

[4] Quoted by Jung in CW 14, ¶49.

out, let me out!" He dug down among the roots of the tree and found a well-sealed glass bottle from which, clearly, the voice had come. He opened it and instantly a spirit rushed out and soon became half as high as the tree. The spirit cried in an awful voice: "I have had my punishment and I will be revenged! I am the great and mighty spirit Mercurius, and now you shall have your reward. Whoso releases me, him I must strangle."[5]

So as soon as the boy sets the spirit free it threatens to destroy him. A person has to be very clever to transform it into something valuable. The story goes on:

This made the boy uneasy and, quickly thinking up a trick, he said, "First I must be sure that you are the same spirit that was shut up in that little bottle." To prove this, the spirit crept back into the bottle. Then the boy made haste to seal it and the spirit was caught again. But now the spirit promised to reward him richly if the boy would let him out. So he let him out and received as a reward a small piece of rag. Quoth the spirit: "If you spread one end of this over a wound it will heal, and if you rub steel or iron with the other end it will turn into silver." Thereupon the boy rubbed his damaged axe with the rag, and the axe turned to silver and he was able to sell it for [a lot of money]. Thus father and son were freed from all worries. The young man could return to his studies, and later, thanks to his rag, he became a famous doctor.

The boy in the story is very canny. He possesses a kind of street-smarts

---

[5] This and following material paraphrased by Jung in CW 13, ¶239. Brackets mine.

of the spirit that makes it possible for him to avoid being destroyed by the power of what he has innocently unleashed. In ordinary reality this level of psychological intelligence is rare.

On my desk is a note that says, "Too young, too naive, too dangerous." I wrote it to myself in the wake of the tragic death of Diana Spencer who, at age 36, could not have achieved the maturity necessary to carry the numinosity she embodied in the way she lived her life. As I see it, the former princess was destroyed by the dark side of the spirit, which she let out of the bottle by leaving the royal family and setting out to live an individual life. If she had remained within the shelter of conventional institutions, the privileges of her station would have been likely to protect her from the conditions that led to her death. It is extraordinarily dangerous for a person who is too idealistically innocent to abandon the collective roles, sanctions, and protections to be found in church or temple, the university, a professional identity, the family, or even a traditional marriage. Yet we live in a time when institutions are breaking down and many people feel compelled to do just that, propelled by what Jung called the archetype of individuation, the instinct to become whole individuals rather than just cogs in a societal machine.

Diana's descent from royalty is a singularly symbolic event, a virtual incarnation of the divine impulse in the collective psyche at this time in history. Ready or not, as we begin the countdown to a new millennium, the power once attributed to God alone is pouring into the general human psyche. Two thousand years ago, Jesus, a single human being, bore the burden of divinity for many. In today's world that same power is often carried by celebrities—kings and princesses, presidents and dictators, cult-leaders and gurus, larger-than-life cultural leaders like Freud and Jung, sports stars, rock musicians, movie stars, and computer moguls. We give divine authority to our physicians, teachers, therapists, parents, spouses, and particularly our children. We experience the power of God in such saviors as science, psychotherapy, Jungianism, democracy, liberalism, ecology, and capitalism, and in phenomena like UFOs and crop circles. Increasingly, however, the power of the Judeo-Christian God-image manifests in the psyches of ordinary people who have no special claim to fame. The spirit is out of the bottle on a large scale, and few are prepared to deal with it. Many people as young and psychologically naive as Diana are unconsciously driven by numinous images and energies that have lost their containers.

• • •

In my imagination, the spirit released from the bottle looks like a mushroom cloud. My psyche seizes on August 6, 1945, when the first nuclear bomb was dropped on Hiroshima, as the moment when the power of God was released from traditional containers and began to pour into contemporary life. Don DeLillo, in the novel *Underworld*,[6] also looks to this event as the source of a profound discontinuity in the American culture.

I do not personally remember Hiroshima, but I do recall the end of the war, eight days after "The Bomb" was dropped. Exuberant crowds filled the streets of every city in this country, even the sleepy farming community of my childhood. To a 12-year-old, the scene was both terrifying and infinitely exciting. Remembering it today brings to mind the dream of a patient many years later, the dream at the front of this book that tells of gods pouring out of the heavens and filling the streets of all the cities and towns in the world. Like the events of that day in 1945, the dream speaks of the perilous and electrifying moment when the power of God enters the human psyche.

• • •

---

[6] New York: Scribner, 1997.

TO BEGIN

I am working at the word-processor in my office. Just as I write, "when the power of God enters the human psyche," something thuds against a window in the adjoining glassed-in porch. I go outside and find a young falcon lying upside down with his feet in the air. I am horrified. The religious side of me is constantly attuned to the symbolic import of what happens in my life, and I feel as I would if something quintessential, perhaps even the holy spirit, had come to grief while trying to enter my house. I touch the bird carefully with my foot. He does not respond, but I can see that he is breathing. I turn him over and caress his feathers, longing for him to live. Suddenly he opens his eyes. When he sees me he lurches frantically, then takes precarious wing and flies to the lowest branch of a nearby fir.

Motionless and nearly invisible, the bird shelters himself against the bark of the tree. I watch him through binoculars. After a minute or two he makes some tentative movements, facing first one way, then the other, on the branch. Something—a foot or a wing—appears to hurt him and he stops moving. He is alert, however, and is still there several hours later, scanning the environment in the way that falcons do. Perhaps he will survive.

Before lunch I take another look. The falcon's back is turned to me and just as I get the binoculars into focus he lifts his tail and defecates. I laugh. On the level of literal reality, I see the movement as a sign of renewed health. Symbolically, I experience the gesture as an expression of something I have had to learn many times, that the gods have no respect for my human concerns. After a moment the falcon flies to the ground, then to a different tree, and a higher branch. I marvel at the radiance of his glossy dark back and white leggings in the sunlight. Finally he flies away.

Just before sunset I see him once again. He is perched on a high branch, targeting the songbirds at my feeder as if he had never been interrupted.

• • •

A single dramatic event, such as Hiroshima, can be no more than a marker of something in the collective psyche whose earliest stirrings are impossible to detect. We could just as well talk about Jonestown, Waco, Oklahoma City, the assassination of John F. Kennedy, or the Nazi Holocaust. We could even go back to Nietzsche's pronouncement that God is dead. "The Bomb" is an unusually potent symbol, however, one that has been incorporated into the vocabulary of contemporary dreams and culture.

In a dream, a nuclear explosion often signals a major and irrevocable change in the consciousness of the dreamer. The decision to drop "The Bomb" on Hiroshima altered something fundamental. Nothing would ever be the same again.

A novel by Chaim Potok, *The Book of Lights*, tells the story of Arthur, the son of a man who was involved in the building of "The Bomb." In one scene, Arthur tells a friend about a childhood memory:

> After the bomb went off, there were sections around Los Alamos where it rained dead birds. I saw more than a dozen birds fall into our yard. They made faint thudding sounds. I was looking out the window and saw them fall. It was pure chance that I saw them. Pure chance, dear Gershon. I remember what they looked like. They smelled charred. Their eyes were burned out. You know, sometimes I think I don't mind it too much that we will probably kill ourselves. We're a terrible species. But we're going to kill all the birds, too.[7]

• • •

---

[7] New York: Knopf, 1981, p. 279.

Normally I do not get wrapped up in the lives of celebrities. I do not even watch television or read a daily newspaper, but rely on my husband David and the incidental input of patients and friends to let me know when something important has happened. If you had asked, I would have said that Diana Spencer meant nothing to me. It made no sense to me that when I heard about her death, I wept.

The next day I awoke feeling stunned, filled with a vague, debilitating, and incomprehensible sense of grief. The malaise mystified me, and so did the pain in my left shoulder that began the following day. It did not occur to me that these things could have anything to do with Diana.

The pain got worse and I made an appointment for a massage. Since I have found that physical problems almost always have a psychological aspect, I also reflected about what meaning a pain in the shoulder might have. Perhaps, I thought, I am trying to carry something too heavy on my shoulders. When I looked it up in a good symbol dictionary I learned that the shoulder is "the highest valued part of a sacrificial animal, to be given to priests and kings of divine authority," and that the shoulder blade is "often consulted for divination."[8] My symptoms were surely speaking to me, but the language was as obscure as that of an ancient oracle. I was not ready to see that, in spite of myself, I was grieving about the death of a woman who had carried an abundance of "divine authority" on her shoulders.

Illumination did not come easily. On Saturday I was barely aware that there was a state funeral in Westminster Abbey, but I was forced to pay my respects unconsciously, immobilized with an icepack on my shoulder. On the seventh day, David and I discussed the week's events

---

[8] Ad de Vries, *Dictionary of Symbols and Imagery* (Amsterdam: Elsevier Science Publishers B.V., 1974).

over a leisurely Sunday breakfast and the light finally dawned.

"My God! Diana!" I said. "I am in mourning for Diana!"

In retrospect, it is hard to understand why I imagined I would not be affected by such a major event in the collective psyche. Diana Spencer was not just a personage, she was a living religious symbol whose death had reverberations throughout the world. The shock waves disturbed the psychological atmosphere as profoundly as a nuclear accident poisons the air. Not only had Diana been a princess, she had *stopped* being a princess. Like God incarnating in a human body, she descended from on high to live in the world of ordinary reality and be the vulnerable person she was, a gutsy, outspoken, independent, passionate, imperfect woman struggling to live her unique life as best she could. Paradoxically, I believe that Diana's descent from royalty made her more numinous than princesshood did, for the impulse to abandon preordained roles for the sake of individual wholeness is a dominant image in the collective psyche today. Because she represented this vital and magnificent potential in all of us she became, in her dying, an object of worship for millions.

One of the most startling aspects of the worldwide mourning for Diana is that it virtually eclipsed the passing of Mother Teresa, an officially-sanctioned holy woman believed by many to have been a living saint. I should not be surprised, however, for it illustrates one of the premises of the chapters that follow—the energy of divinity is rarely where we expect it to be. We find it where we feel it, and we often feel it in people, places, objects, and events that we deem too trivial, contemptible, threatening, irrational, or just plain odd to take seriously.

• • •

The word *god* comes from the Indo-European root *gheu(e)* which means "to call; invoke." As roots go, *gheu(e)* is quite simple. It has only three variants, comprising two branches. One branch simply means "god," and has two variants, *god*, and the English name *Godfrey*. The third cognate, of which the whole second branch consists, is *giddy*. It comes from a Germanic root that means "possessed by a god; insane."[9]

It pays to remember what an intimate connection there is between divinity and insanity.

---

[9] William Morris (ed.), *The American Heritage Dictionary of the English Language*, with appendix listing Indo–European roots (Boston: Houghton Mifflin, 1981).

chapter two

THE CALLING
OF OLIVER NOVAK

Should not . . . God himself be allowed to speak, despite our only
too understandable fear of the primary experience?
—C. G. JUNG[1]

No one in his right mind chooses to be a vessel for raw God-energy. It is a matter of being called or chosen, often in a way so bizarre and socially unacceptable that the last thing you want to do is talk about it, even to your analyst. Several sessions went by before Oliver told me he had done time, as a youngster, in one of those small, private mental hospitals for the very rich. I found it hard to believe that this gentle, engaging young introvert had ever been crazy. Oliver's kooky sense of humor tickled me, and I warmed to his intrepid spirit. His overlong legs, bright blue eyes and short-cropped yellow hair reminded me more of a newborn chicken than a madman.

---

[1] Letter to Oskar Schmitz in *Psychological Perspectives*, spring, 1975, p. 82.

Appearances can deceive, however, and I was a little worried. The first dream a patient brings to analysis is likely to contain the key to his psychology, and Oliver's initial dream had shocked and frightened me:

> *Screams are coming out of my mouth. At the same time, a great stream of "death and filth" is coming forth from a rotten and decaying hole in the center of my head.*

As Edinger has pointed out, "Dreams that emphasize blackness usually occur when the conscious ego is one-sidedly identified with the light."[2] I believed this to be true for Oliver, but could not imagine what gruesome things could be in his unconscious, waiting to come screaming out.

My patient's presenting symptom—the thing that had motivated him to find an analyst—was a compulsion to wear women's clothes. He tried to stick to underwear, but the impulse overtook him at unexpected moments and he was terrified of being caught. In the early 1970s, cultural attitudes were nearly universally intolerant of atypical gender behavior. Oliver would surely have lost his position in the justice system, working with delinquent adolescents, if anyone had discovered that he cross-dressed. Otherwise, however, the symptom seemed harmless enough, and the magnitude of his fear puzzled me.

"Why don't you tell your wife?" I asked. "It would be safer to do it at home."

Oliver stared at me. His face turned so white I thought he was going to faint.

"I can't tell Myra," he said. "She might not understand."

Gradually his story came out. At age 14, Oliver had been fascinated by the dresses hanging on a neighbor's clothesline. One day he filched one

---

[2] Edward F. Edinger, *Anatomy of the Psyche* (La Salle, IL: Open Court, 1985), p. 150.

and put it on. His mother caught him wearing it, was horrified, and took him to a psychiatrist. The doctor persuaded her to hospitalize her son and authorize electroshock therapy, which achieved its purpose with a vengeance. Oliver made no more attempts to cross-dress.

Now, however, twenty years later, the impulse had returned.

I was aghast. Electroconvulsive therapy was an extreme treatment, more so than today, because the doses of electric shock were higher.

"Are you telling me you were given electroshock just because you wanted to wear a skirt?"

He nodded. I looked down at the trousers I was wearing and shuddered.

"Didn't you have other symptoms? Hallucinations? Crazy ideas?"

Oliver shook his head. "Not that I remember. My mother was really upset about the clothes. She thought it meant I was crazy."

Later I would hear about many abuses of the mental health system, but at the time I found it hard to believe what I was hearing. In fact, I was beside myself. I could do nothing to change the past, however, but could try to find out whether and how the damage could be repaired. Oliver's psyche was already working on this problem, and I gradually realized that his impulse to cross-dress was the first step in his healing process. The parts of himself that had been amputated years before were trying to return.

In many societies, men with special spiritual authority are expected to wear skirts. Roman Catholic and Episcopal priests in our own culture wear dresses as vestments. Similarly, the shamans of some tribal groups are seen as a special class of men "similar to women."[3] A man who is called to serve the tribe in this way can be condemned to death if he refuses.[4]

---

[3] Mircea Eliade, *Shamanism* (Princeton, NJ: Princeton University Press, 1964), p. 258.

[4] *Shamanism*, p. 351.

Edinger describes the sea goddess Ino's rescue of Odysseus from a terrible storm by telling the hero to take off his clothes and swim to shore. She gives him her veil to wear, saying that it is enchanted and will protect him from harm. Edinger suggests that Ino's veil may be the archetypal image behind transvestism: "The veil represents the support and containment which the mother archetype can provide the ego during a dangerous activation of the unconscious."[5]

Oliver's unconscious was indeed activated, and his psyche gradually prepared him for the coming storm. First, a spirit animal came to him in a dream:

> *I am standing in a still, quiet pool, up to my neck in water. An otter pops up about three feet from me. He shakes the water off, looks at me with great intelligence, then looks across the pond at a bridge-like structure. His eyes are filled with meaning. I reach over and touch him, scratching him lightly, tentatively. I can feel the bristliness of his hair.*

This odd and gentle dream touched me deeply, stirring a remote and primal place inside. I stored it in a niche in my psyche reserved for such treasures, keeping it safe until I could find a way to look at it that satisfied me. Years later I found the key to its meaning in Mircea Eliade's book on shamanism.

> In the beginning, that is, in mythical times, man lived at peace with the animals and understood their speech. It was not until after a primordial catastrophe, comparable to the "Fall" of Biblical tradition, that man became what he is today—mortal, sexed, obliged to work to feed himself, and at enmity with the

---

[5] Edward F. Edinger, *Ego and Archetype* (Baltimore: Penguin, 1973), p. 115.

animals. While preparing for his ecstasy and during it, the shaman abolishes the present human condition and, for the time being, recovers the situation as it was at the beginning.[6]

In that sense, Oliver was preparing to go back to the beginning. He was moving toward an earlier, more primitive psychological state that lived in him before he suffered the "civilizing" effects of shock therapy.

The next week, in the only dream he remembered, Oliver saw an old, old woman. The week after that he dreamed:

My hair has grown very, very long, down past my waist.

Sometimes a single image is easier to understand than the elaborate narratives we tend to think of as "real dreams." When a remembered dream is fragmentary, the part that is recalled often appears to be packed with essential meaning, just as a sketchy early memory often captures the essence of a person's psychology. In a way, Oliver's dream of growing long hair told the whole story. It was as if electroshock had cut off much of what grew naturally out of his head, but now his thoughts and fantasies were growing unchecked and his psychological locks had become as flowing and full as if they had never been shorn.

Like transvestism, long hair has both feminine and spiritual connotations. It may also allude to the ecstasy that helps the long-haired shaman ascend and magically fly.[7]

Oliver's ecstasy was less than a month in coming. A dream prefigured it and was soon followed by a phone call from his wife Myra. In the dream:

I am visiting a man doctor in the office of what is usually a woman doctor. He

---

[6] *Shamanism*, p. 99.
[7] *Shamanism*, p. 407.

is a little stuffy but it is a good hour. As I am leaving I decide not to use my feet. I grasp the handrail and sort of float down the steps to the ground. At the bottom we all talk about it a bit. It is OK. No harm.

I guessed that the image of the doctor might refer to me, and gathered that I had been a bit pedantic the hour before, speaking from the masculine side of myself that Jung calls the animus. I wondered if my stuffiness were instrumental in Oliver's decision to leave the ground.

In the phone call, Myra said her husband was having a rather unusual experience, and asked for an appointment to talk about it. "Soon, please," she said, and laughed. "I think it may be urgent."

Myra turned out to be quite different from the woman Oliver had described. This is not unusual. I have learned to take what a patient says about a spouse with a grain of salt, because such descriptions often say more about the person's own inner images of woman or man—the anima or animus—than about the partner's objective reality. The woman Oliver imagined was someone who, like his mother, would not be able to handle his cross-dressing. In contrast, the real Myra was just what the doctor ordered. A tough-minded but compassionate woman several years Oliver's senior, she was not fazed by the gentle psychotic state into which he had fallen, and was prepared to stay with him day and night and take full responsibility for his safety. Above all, she said, he must not be hospitalized, a prospect that filled him with horror.

"Yes," I said, "I understand. No hospital. And what are his symptoms?"

She laughed. "Well," she said, "mainly he wants to fuck everything that walks and some things that don't. We're spending a lot of time in bed and I'm watching him like a hawk to keep him out of trouble with the law. I called in sick for him, but I don't suppose excuses will work forever."

A psychiatrist prescribed tiny doses of antipsychotic medication, and Myra brought her husband to see me every other day for the two weeks the episode lasted. For me, it was a strange and wonderful experience. Erotic energy filled the room like a warm bath, but my authority as Oliver's analyst was great enough that he did not try to act out his sexual impulses with me. I imagined that the sexuality pouring out of his psyche embodied the "death and filth" that flowed from the center of his head as if from a lanced boil in his initial dream. "How tragic," I thought, "that he was given so black a view of his sexuality that he had to lock it up for all those years."

In the mythic descriptions of transmutation that found a voice in ancient alchemy, images of death and filth as *mortificatio* (killing) and *putrefactio* (rotting) allude to essential aspects of the process of psychological change. A dream early in Oliver's breakdown reassured me that his *mortificatio*, which amounted to a total eclipse of the ego, had a constructive purpose:

> *A very young aspect of me is traveling by foot over the face of the earth, which is being transformed by great earth-moving machinery. I am a child among the earthmovers.*

My patient's psyche was clearly going through a major process of reconstruction. His job was to stay out of the gigantic machinery's way and try not to get hurt.

In another dream the same night, Oliver was an actor in a movie, playing the role of Marilyn Monroe, one of our culture's incarnations of the goddess of love. The film was a great success and Oliver had many fans. Later in the dream he hired someone else to play the part while he became director and producer. The dream hinted that one purpose of what he was going through might be to celebrate and reconnect him to his natural eroticism. His later role as director and producer suggested that in time Oliver's ego would be able to reclaim its rightful role as director of the drama in which his psyche had involved him, instead of indiscriminately acting out the raw eroticism symbolized by Marilyn Monroe.

An unusually long and detailed dream marked the end of Oliver's brief psychotic episode and revealed its fundamentally religious nature: The dream is set in the church service of an unknown denomination. At the beginning the congregation is divided in two, with Oliver at the center front of the righthand section and another man, "the deacon," in the corresponding position on the lefthand side. The minister and two assistants stand at the front of the center aisle where the altar normally is in an outer-world church.

The divided church in which Oliver finds himself is, I believe, an image of the Judeo-Christian aspect of his psyche, split because it lays claim to good but not evil, spirit but not nature, masculine but not feminine, Christ but not Antichrist. The minister and his two assistants may allude to the Christian trinity.

Oliver's position at the center of the righthand section shows his onesided identification with goodness and light, which his initial dream had already revealed. This bias is common in our culture, but Oliver's antipathy to "the other side" is exceptionally rigid because his socialization had happened in such a traumatic way. The dream's church service seems to be a metaphor for his present breakdown, and is designed to remedy his onesidedness by giving elements from both sides of the psyche an opportunity to move. In Oliver's words:

A person on the aisle on the left-hand side sings long passages in response to the minister's sung calls. At the same time he moves rapidly about the congregation, always returning to his place at the end of the passage. His hands are held out to his sides at elbow height, palms down. He looks like a very dignified, white-haired small boy doing bombing runs in the congregation!

As the ceremony continues, Oliver begins to sing in response to the calls sung by the minister. Then he and the other members of the congregation join the first man in swooping about with their arms held out from the elbows, wandering further and further through the church as they do so. Among the participants is someone Oliver describes as "a glazed-looking young fellow from the back who looks like a central-casting selection for 'young hayseed from small midwest town,'" an apt personification of Oliver's ingenuousness. As Oliver begins to enjoy swooping and wandering about, he says he feels "like Peter O'Toole in 'The Ruling Class,' when he's found his congregation and is expressing his calling as Jesus Christ and has this great transfigured look on his face, with his misty blue eyes."

At the high point of the ceremony the deacon takes off and begins moving out of the main body into the side vestibules and the nave, singing "Glory to God, Halleluia." Later the deacon interrupts the service to shout at Oliver, "There's no fringe benefits, you know. They don't deduct social security or income tax." Oliver concludes that the whole thing has been an employment interview and that, without quite knowing what he's gotten into, he's been hired.

He gets into an argument with the deacon about whether his annuity will be deducted before or after he claims income for income tax. In his words:

I bet the deacon a beer that I'm right, he ups it to two, then three. Meanwhile I'm working at the church. Finally during one ceremony the deacon glares at me and shouts in the middle of a response: 'Thirteen!' That was the number of beers we'd gotten up to. That day I go to the various tax attorneys in town and give each of them a postcard to send the deacon. Except for the signature, the postcards are all the same. They say, 'Deacon—Oliver is right.' Then he and I go down to the tavern, and I can't drink thirteen beers by myself so we drink them together.

The deacon is a pivotal figure. As leader of the lefthand side, he represents something that actively opposes Oliver's conscious attitude. The reference to number 13 suggests that he may be an advocate of the devil, possibly even the devil himself. Perhaps he embodies the force within Oliver that compels him to cross-dress, an impulse that he experiences as diabolical, *i.e.*, beyond the pale of acceptability.

The number 13 has archetypal links not only to the devil, but also to nature, to the Great Goddess, and to wholeness. The disastrous consequences of Oliver's first experiment in transvestism had imbued him with the patriarchal bias of a culture that regards both nature and the feminine as somewhat demonic. Now, however, he learns that he must consume large quantities of the natural, earthy spirit of the beer. This should make him less one-sided and bring him closer to his own wholeness.

The swooping and wandering movements of the rather Dionysian church service, as well as the responsive singing, provide the occasion for people to intermingle. It is as if the ceremony's entire purpose is to weave the two sides together into a unified whole. Indeed, even though Oliver calls upon the authority of the law to prove that he is right, the deacon has to help him drink the thirteen beers. That is, Oliver cannot assimilate his winnings without the help of his adversary. He does not exactly make a pact with the devil, but the two of them come to a definite understanding.

Eventually the whole order of the congregation is rearranged, the minister dies, and Oliver is given the minister's living quarters. He is assigned two desks, which he has to locate by their serial numbers. One, he says, "contains the handwritten, before-printing-press versions of the *Index Medicus*—the complete series, from number 1 up to the advent of the printing press." These volumes now belong to Oliver, and when he finds the desk where they are stored he wakes up.

Being given the place once occupied by the minister puts Oliver in charge of his individual religious experience. He can no longer leave it in the hands of the traditional authority symbolized by the minister. In fact, the whole church service turns out to have been an employment interview, in the course of which he was repeatedly "called," *i.e.*, given his vocation. Rivkah Kluger points out that, seen psychologically, the religious idea of being called refers to the awakening of individual identity, when a person is "removed from the anonymous existence in the cycle of nature and placed into a personal, unique fate."[8] Once called, an individual must live in conscious relation to the God-image in the psyche, the organizing center that Jung named the Self. To turn away can be extremely dangerous.[9] The dresses beckoning to Oliver from his neighbor's clothesline were probably the first instrument of his calling.

In the dream, Oliver's vocation unfolds gradually, culminating in the inheritance of a guide to all the medical knowledge up to the middle of the 15th century, when the printing press was invented. The 15th and 16th centuries were a watershed in the history of the Western psyche, when a conflict arose between divine revelation and scientific knowledge, a rift between Mother Church and Mother Nature. If the *Index Medicus* had existed then, it would have contained only ecclesiastical writings, a hint that what Oliver has inherited concerns the spiritual side of the healing process. The dream as a whole is one of the clearest statements I have seen that *the psyche views as religious certain events that modern medicine labels psychotic.*

It would be misleading to suggest that this remarkable dream was the end of the matter. Oliver's was a lifetime assignment, and the dream he

---

[8] Rivkah S. Kluger, *Psyche and Bible* (Zurich: Spring Publications, 1974), p. 19.
[9] For an example see Edward F. Edinger, *The Bible and the Psyche* (Toronto: Inner City Books, 1986), p. 49.

brought to our last session, seven months later, did not speak of peaceful resolution:

I am observing myself. There are two Olivers, face to face, struggling with each other.

Having learned to stand aside and reflect upon the war within him, without repressing either side of the conflict, Oliver was drafted into the service of what Jung calls today's religious task, the "creative confrontation with the opposites and their synthesis in the self, the wholeness of the personality."[10]

Not everyone is called as dramatically as Oliver, but many are. The sad thing is that modern medicine, keeper of the *contemporary* volumes of the *Index Medicus,* is so unaware of the purpose and meaning of psychological symptoms that it regularly tries to excise its greatest ally in the healing process, the patient's own psyche. I once heard the story of a suicidally-depressed woman who had been diagnosed manic-depressive and treated with lithium. Kathy was a practicing Catholic and had two therapists, a psychiatrist to monitor her medication and a priest with whom she talked about her problems. One day when she was with the priest, she heard God speak. He told her she was a valuable human being and gave her permission not to kill herself. Naturally her depression lifted. At first she kept the message from God to herself, and the sudden improvement looked like a miracle to her family and friends. Then she told the psychiatrist about it. He told her she was delusional and persuaded her to commit herself to a hospital, where the urge to kill herself returned and she again became trapped in a cycle of despair, pills, and periodic confinement.

• • •

---

[10] C. G. Jung, *Memories, Dreams, Reflections* (New York: Random House, 1961), p. 338.

The memory of my experience with Oliver, in such contrast to tragedies like Kathy's, encouraged me to undertake an experiment, from 1985 to 1989, in the small community in which I live. A dozen or so concerned individuals offered around-the-clock emotional support and protection from physical harm to a few people who wanted to make their way through the maze of psychological breakdown at home, with little or no medication. We called the project Tamanawas, a name derived from the Chinookan language family of the Pacific Northwest, meaning "shaman," "shaman magic," and "guardian spirit." A Native word was chosen because tribal cultures are more mindful than ours of the natural healing process that often lies behind psychotic symptoms.

The people of Tamanawas undertook to midwife eight breakdowns involving seven patients. Two episodes had to be stopped with medication before the process was complete, one a child whose special needs we were not equipped to handle. All the adults are functioning well today and some are making major contributions in professional and creative fields. None are free of pain or symptoms, but who is? Some look back at their Tamanawas experience with gratitude and affection, others with regret, anguish, or anger.

I asked both patients and caretakers to write about their perceptions of Tamanawas, the bad parts as well as the good. The following stories convey the flavor of what happened and the strikingly individual charac-ter of each person's experience.

• • •

Nick, a caretaker, says, "In all the sessions I was part of, I was healed along with the patient. Every opportunity to be a caretaker was a chance to face the unconscious and learn about myself. Sometimes I felt guilty that I got so much enjoyment and growth from the sessions. I thought

'Wait a minute. Shouldn't I be standing aloof, watching and advising? What am I doing here in the thick of things?' But my task *was* to participate, to be a guide and anchor in the 'real world' while entering as fully into their 'crazy world' as I could. In this way they became guides for me as well, leading me around in the unfamiliar territory of the unconscious.

"I accepted no money for my time as a caretaker. The world revealed in someone else's madness was too fascinating for me not to feel that I was being adequately compensated for my time just by being there.

"One time I sat with Carla in the middle of the night, together with Melanie. Each of us had to meet the client's approval before we could serve as their caretaker, and my approval came when I went to Carla's house and knocked on the door. After a long time a woman came to the door, took my hand and led me into the living room where other caretakers were sitting. One of them pointed to the woman who had my hand and said, 'that's Carla.' I was surprised, first that she would be allowed to come to the door, second that she was so friendly and nonaggressive. I had been warned that she could be somewhat threatening, but at no time during the eight hours I spent with her was she in the least angry or threatening.

"Much of that night is shaky in my memory and a lot like a dream. Whenever I try to pin down a detail, it changes somehow, but the feeling tone stays with me clearly—positive, warm, and powerful. There was power and importance in everything the three of us did. It was clear that what we were doing, however odd, was crucial."

• • •

Laura has had several breakdowns. During the one she began with Tamanawas she made an attempt to throw herself through a closed second-story window. At that point the decision was made to interrupt the process and take her to the hospital for antipsychotic medication. She writes:

"My experience at Tamanawas was terrible. All of my psychotic experiences have been terrible beyond belief, each worse than the last. From hindsight I see the experience at Tamanawas as damaging to my ongoing life, which the first hospitalization was not. This is because of the phone call when I screamed at my mother from a psychotic state. This continues to have repercussions in my relationships with my family, and I regret profoundly that it happened. I regret also that a friend was with me, someone who did not understand psychosis and who was left alone with me and made the decision not to interfere with the phone call. I should not have had a phone available while in that state, and I should not have been left in the sole care of a friend.

"Other than that, my impressions are mixed. For me nature is healing, and at the beginning of my time at Tamanawas I was able to be outside in nature. One excellent woman was with me outside and her presence was calming for me. I bounced quickly between inner and outer experience, both very intense. I was like a brain-damaged child; my senses were too alert, or I was unable to filter them, and I became confused by so many things around me. But it was the people who had the strongest effect. Too many of them wanted to do a good job, seemed excited and motivated by the desire to perform. I remember wishing they would leave me alone. They were so committed to keeping me unmedicated that it took hours for me to get them to agree to take me for medication. My sense of time was disrupted, but I remember longing to have a chemical release and feeling unable to get attended to.

"This is my current response to the Tamanawas experience. But there is something else. Less than two months later I was able to take on a new job, in a new profession where I needed to stand behind my own convictions, often in conflict with other professionals. Also, throughout the previous ten years I had increasingly experienced terror. In some settings it was so extreme that it occurred about every ten minutes, and took an enormous amount of energy to cope with. While I was not free of terror [after the Tamanawas experience], I did get freed from ongoing and non-specific terror. It is no longer a condition of my life, in the way that it was. I don't know whether there's a causal relationship between Tamanawas and these changes.

"Recently I had a moment when for the first time I relied on, was almost glad for, my psychotic experiences. Someone told me about two brief and terrible experiences that were like 'brief psychotic episodes.' I felt the ground rising under my feet to be supportive, to hold it at some distance, begin to manage it, and seek appropriate help. So for a moment I was grateful and able to see myself in a new light."

• • •

Stacy has a different perspective on Laura's episode:

"I came after work for what I expected to be the first of several days of caretaking Laura, but she had decided to end her drug free journey into the unconscious, so Melanie and I escorted her to the hospital to receive an antipsychotic drug to stop the process. I let Melanie lead the way, as she had more experience and a good sense about how to move and communicate in the terrain of the unconscious.

"We arrived at the hospital late at night and waited to be admitted. We had to keep talking to Laura, reassuring her that she wasn't bad, or a disappointment [for stopping the process].

"Two critical things happened. Laura left to go to an exam room while Melanie and I waited in the lobby. Melanie was uncomfortable with this and went to the door to the hallway Laura had gone down. Just then Laura came bounding out, confused and determined to leave. She had become very fearful. I'm sure the hospital scene alarmed her and she was getting further and further into it. That decided it—we all went to her exam room and had to struggle to restrain her from tearing her hair out and bashing her head. Sometimes she was calm. She seemed sure her children were dead and it was her fault and this made her 'crazy.' A very nervous intern came in, shaking but trying to control himself. He asked us if we knew how serious this was, as we all seemed quite ordinary about it. We said we knew, and that things were all right, but she wanted antipsychotics. He said things were *not* all right, dangerous even, and what made us say things were okay?

"Melanie said 'We do know and we are very serious.' He said, 'Talk to me.' Simply and quickly she explained what Tamanawas was and what we were trying to do. She said we offered an opportunity for people with psychotic episodes to try to work through the material in a safe and protected environment; that we had been with her for several days; and that she had come to the point of asking to be admitted to a hospital and receive antipsychotics. The intern said, 'Then she has been in the very best situation possible.' He stopped shaking and reached out to Laura and told her she was in good hands and everything would be okay. I could see *he* was in good hands, too. This was the second critical moment, because if he had not listened, the chain of events could have taken a very different turn. He said he would keep the psychiatrist from coming in to examine her while she was in the midst of her 'ravings,' or surely she would be committed to a mental care facility and it would take court action to release her! We were *that* close. He administered the drug and we stayed with her until she became coherent again.

"Later it dawned on me how critical this intern's part was. He stood at the crossroads and made the decision that made things simple. Otherwise it would have taken a long and painful court proceeding for Laura's family to regain custody of her. I was grateful to him, and to Melanie for communicating with him at the right time in the right way. I was in awe of the way it went.

"The effect on me lasted for days. I had to call and talk to Melanie for hours the first few nights. She called it contamination—not in the disease sense, but in having been touched deeply, my unconscious mixed up with Laura's, Laura's spilling over into mine. And that is what it felt like. I was scared and disoriented. I felt like I had been falling, falling, and when I stopped to look around, I didn't recognize much. I was rearranged. Things didn't fit together in the usual way and the possibilities of meaning in the world were staggering. Melanie and I just kept talking about it until I felt calm. And then I'd call her the next night and do the same thing. We went over the whole experience until I could feel my feet back on the ground again.

"I remember thinking how out of control it seemed. What were we doing? Who did we think we were? What made any of us think we could do this work? What horrendous chances were we taking? The whole thing seemed to have been riding on a thin edge. I think it really *was* riding on a thin edge, not because we were irresponsible, but because it is the nature of the work. We hadn't created a situation that was out of control, but the psychotic episode *is* wild and mostly unknown, and it requires, besides experience, a good deal of intuition about what to say and do. A circumstance in which everyone is operating on intuition is wild and unusual, and I came to understand that most of what I felt uncomfortable about had to do with my lack of experience with situations like that. When I understood that, I was less concerned with what was unknown about the work and more impressed with how much everyone *was* able to do.

"I was both sorry and relieved when it was over. It was *so* demanding I was glad to return to my normal little life, but it was so exciting to learn so much and stretch my boundaries that it was worth the overextension I felt. We never took care of another client after that, so I never got to do any more work of this kind. I would do it again in a minute, and hoped and feared I would be called.

"I felt that one of the limitations of Tamanawas was that we were doing something beyond the usual scope of our cultural, historical, and spiritual experience—trying to make sense of and be guides through psychotic territory. Impossible without the work of Carl Jung—very, very, difficult for newcomers to the work. I do not doubt that the approach we were taking was *at least* coming from the right direction. Only a longer history of doing it would show just how appropriate it was.

"The training for Tamanawas was helpful, but my years of dream work with a therapist were what really laid the ground. Without that, I would have been too unprepared."

• • •

Sarah's breakdown was quite different from Laura's. So is her feeling about it today. She says:

"Tamanawas worked for me. That's a simple, blunt sentence, yet it contains a lot! My gratitude is ever-present. Looking through my breakdown notes is still a potent experience. I cry as I read them.

"Therapy was *most important*. A breakdown can't be a single miracle event—at least not for me. I do suggest that caregivers refrain from saying, 'I know exactly what you mean, I had a dream just like that,' and from defining another person's experience.

"I don't seem able to explain or describe Tamanawas—except that it works and it makes sense. The Tamanawas project has not ended for me. It has just become internal.

I am doing well. Thinking about law school. Thank you for your work with me. Now I know of my worth and courage."

• • •

Although the work of Tamanawas came to an end, its spirit is very much alive. There is a great deal to be learned, but when the religious aspect of the psyche is understood deeply enough by enough people to provide a matrix of cultural support, I believe the Tamanawas model could provide a humane and practical addition or alternative to conventional treatments for acute psychosis. I hope it will be the way of the future.

I am often asked whether the healing from this kind of work is permanent, or whether psychosis recurs. My experience is limited, and the people with whom I have worked in this way have all been highly motivated, intelligent, and able to self-reflect—after the episode, if not during it. Also, each of them worked analytically with me for a time after recovery, to understand and integrate their experience. Laura is the only one I know of for whom psychosis has recurred. She differed from others in the group in several ways, all of which may be important variables: Her Tamanawas experience took place in a community other than her own; she had been hospitalized and/or medicated for several episodes before she tried Tamanawas; her behavior during the Tamanawas episode became dangerous to her; and medication was used to terminate her symptoms.

A factor that I have come to feel may be essential to a successful outcome is a religious attitude, including the capacity to feel and express gratitude for the help received from others and from the healing process in the psyche.

• • •

Two decades after the end of my work with Oliver, his psychotic symptoms have not recurred. He writes to give me permission to tell his story and tell me that he and Myra are busy and content. I am delighted to hear that he has not stopped growing, but continues to make contact with aspects of himself that he did not know he had.

The letter is one of several he has written me over the years. One contains the gift of a poem by Myra and with it, a mandala drawn by Oliver. Another says simply:

"Now that I have sat here for ten minutes wondering how to say anything after telling you how my life is going well and calmly and pleasantly—well, thank you. May your life also be well and calm and pleasant."

Oliver's letters do not mention his work with the justice system. Either his job has changed or it has ceased to be important, existing only to support the creative efforts that are the true work of his spirit. Neither does he mention the subject of skirts. I wonder if he ever wears them now, as a ritual allowing safe passage to the other side, or if the impulse dropped away like a booster rocket once he was fully launched. I wish I could tell you, but I do not know.

That is how it is for an analyst. You never hear the end of the story. But then, perhaps the inner story of a life *has* no end. People come for help, and you walk with them for a while, and sometimes get to know them more deeply than you feel a person has a right to know another human being. Eventually, when the work goes well, your paths begin to diverge. Then, like the Northwest Indians who return the bones of the sacred salmon, cleaned and blessed, to be reborn, you bid your patient a joyous farewell and give him back to the river.

chapter three

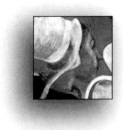

GWILYM*

In the eyes of the alchemists the fire-point, the divine centre in man, was something dangerous, a powerful poison which required very careful handling if it was to be changed into the panacea. The process of individuation, likewise, has its own specific dangers.

—C. G. JUNG[1]

I am cleaning up a pile of scrap lumber in my yard when a garden snake glides out and I am suddenly thrust back in time, fifty years or more, by an image of the trash heap I used to pass on my way to play at Sweezey's pond and woods.

A solitary child, I spent hours and days out of time, exploring the fallow farmland beyond the town limits. When I headed toward the Sweezey property, I always stopped to stare at the rusted metal bed springs, decaying dolls, and archaic whiskey bottles that had been dumped at a spot

---

*This chapter was originally titled "Depth Psychology's Charlatan Shadow," and first appeared in *Quadrant: The Journal of the C. G. Jung Foundation for Analytical Psychology*, published by the C. G. Jung Foundation of New York, © copyright, the C. G. Jung Foundation of New York, 1997. Reprinted by permission.
[1] CW 14, ¶49.

where the path divided. If I were lucky, I might catch a glimpse of one of the snakes that nested there, reptiles of proportions and capacities I have not seen since.

The blue racers took my breath away, long shiny streaks the color of midnight sky. But what I hoped and feared to see more than anything else were the blow snakes, primitive dust-brown adders that puffed themselves up to at least twice their size when threatened.

The other kids said that blow snakes breathed out poisonous vapors. I had my doubts about that, but I kept my distance just in case. Sometimes, as I watched a nest of the eerie creatures ballooning into a fat, ugly tangle, I would feel queasy enough to believe that I had been poisoned, but my parents assured me that Michigan had no poisonous snakes.

When I grew older, my fascination with the denizens of society's dumping grounds assumed a different shape. I did not pursue the literal study of snakes, but the profession of depth psychology has been for me a kind of herpetology of the spirit, wherein fields and forests, trash heaps and serpents take metaphoric form. In my work I find countless opportunities to observe and catalog the unpredictable and sometimes deadly inhabitants of the psyche. My consulting room is the laboratory for such research, while my personal life provides studies in the field.

One of the richest dumps in Western culture contains the mysterious ideas of alchemy, thrown out when the science of chemistry replaced them. It took the genius of Jung to recognize that the true substance of the discarded alchemical texts was psychology, not chemistry. Noticing that similar images appeared in many modern dreams, he began to salvage nuggets of living spirit from alchemy's abstruse symbolism.

In essence, alchemy is a mythology of transformation. Its recipes are metaphors for the processes through which human beings, like snakes shedding their skins, can achieve psychological and spiritual transmutation and enlightenment. The alchemists believed that their highest value, the philosopher's stone, could be refined from disgusting items like feces, urine, and vomit, and that base metals could be turned into gold. Although absurd in literal reality, these ideas express an important psychological truth: the path that leads to integration and wholeness begins by facing the most repugnant parts of ourselves and the most miserable aspects of our lives.

Alchemists whose desire was focused on creating material gold rather than "our gold, which is not the common gold" were considered to be an inferior breed whose work was dangerous and destructive. Because of a reputation for overusing the bellows, they were called "puffers." Their practices caused a great many problems for others. In fact, "In [medieval] England there was so much evidence of confidence-trickery that the performance of alchemical experiments was limited by a system of Royal Licenses,"[2] much as licensing laws today attempt both to regulate the methods used and to curb exaggerated claims by present-day puffers in the healing professions.

As Jungians are fond of pointing out, *everything* casts a shadow, something that Joseph Campbell put clearly when he said that everything we do has both good and evil consequences.[3] This is as true of institutions and professions as it is of individuals. Alchemical puffery prefigured the exploitative, abusive, shadow side of modern psychotherapy, embodied by the archetypal image of the charlatan. *The American Heritage Dictionary* defines a charlatan as "a person who claims to possess knowledge or skill that he does not have," which is to say that the charlatan is "puffed up."

It takes a lot of chutzpah for me to talk about this subject because I have lived my life pushing at the constraints of convention, and as a result

[2] C. A. Burland, *The Arts of the Alchemists* (New York: Macmillan, 1968), p. 66.
[3] *Joseph Campbell and the Power of Myth*, with Bill Moyers (New York: Mystic Fire Video, 1988), 6 tapes.

have made more than my share of professional errors. My training taught me little about the abuse of power or boundary issues between analysts and patients because few people gave much thought to such matters then. The importance and dimensions of these and related ethical issues are only slowly becoming visible to the profession and, like many others, I have had to carve what I know about the dark side of psychotherapy from painful personal experience.

When therapists or analysts overtly pretend to authority, training, credentials, or skills that they lack, the charlatanism is transparent, but the ways in which most of us overstep the boundaries of our competence are less obvious. It happens subtly, often by implication, whenever we fail to recognize our human limits. At bottom the problem of charlatanism is a religious one, in which the boundary between the human and the divine has been erased or become distorted.

Paradoxically, our greatest virtues are often what open the door to the shadow, so to some extent the more perfect we try to be, the worse we become. For instance, analysts tend to be kind, loving, and generous people who want to help. These are clearly benevolent traits, but carried too far, they tempt us to overreach and make promises we cannot keep. At her first appointment with a patient who had repeatedly been abandoned, first by his mother and later by a series of lovers, an analyst says, "*I'll* never leave you!" She wants to relieve his anxiety, but the charlatan has caught her, for life is unpredictable. Plans change, we get sick, we die, and in time this analyst will certainly leave her patient unless he leaves her first. Similarly, in our eagerness to be helpful we offer more and more, not considering whether, in truth, we are objective enough to serve as analyst for someone we have made a friend, student, business partner, or lover. There is hardly a person who does not long for someone to save him from life's painful difficulties, hardly an analyst who can resist the role of savior. We do not like to admit how little any of us really knows about the psyche, how little power we have to relieve human suffering. As a result, like the boy in the fairy tale, we sometimes conjure up bigger spirits than we bargained for.

The privacy of the consulting room offers countless opportunities for an analyst to play God. Depth psychologists, who look into the unconscious and presume to address the needs of the soul, may be particularly susceptible. Although we often use the word *soul* in imprecise and somewhat sentimental ways, Jung had a very clear idea of what he meant by it. He spoke of the soul as an organ of perception. Just as the eye permits us to see light, he said, the soul makes it possible for us to perceive God.[4] That is, the soul responds to what is numinous.

In analysis, numinous levels of the psyche regularly get activated. When a God-image is touched and has nowhere else to go, it commonly lands on the analyst, who becomes numinous to the patient. It is as if the analyst takes on the power and majesty of God. We say that the God-image is projected on the analyst, but the technical terminology does not do justice to the experience. It feels as though something like a powerful magnetic field had entered the room, inducing worshipful feelings and subtly altering the consciousness of everyone present. When this happens, patients become more or less mesmerized, surrendering individual power and judgment in much the same way that cult members are rendered unconscious by the charisma of their leader. This is the stage of analysis when a patient is apt to feel great enthusiasm for everything the analyst says and does, even things he knows are wrong. Unless the analyst sees what is happening—and that level of understanding is rare—she *also* is likely to be stunned by the God-image she is carrying. It is a dangerous moment, when the temptation for an analyst to abuse the power of her position can be overwhelming. There is no immunity. As I see it, the only

---

[4] CW 12, ¶14.

safety lies in consciousness of what is going on, together with careful attention to accepted ethical standards.

Most analysts are decent human beings, striving in good faith to deal responsibly with the psyche's unpredictable power. In that context there is room for the usual amount of human error. Jung rightly said, however, that "medicine in the hands of a fool was ever poison and death,"[5] and the human condition admits of far worse than foolishness. Once in a very great while there appears a person whose character and disregard for standards embody the charlatan to the hilt. I once fell into the hands of someone like that and the experience nearly destroyed me. Shame at having been duped and fear of retaliation silenced me for many years. Now that he is dead, however, and I am in my 60s, I feel it is time to tell the story.

Call him Gwilym. Long after our relationship ended he continued to haunt me in my dreams. Years later, in a desperate attempt to come to terms with his poisonous impact, I undertook what amounts to a psychoanalysis of our work together. Only then could I face the devastation, only then see how inauthentic the ground on which he stood, a kind of psychological quicksand into which I fell, too. In retrospect I believe that Gwil was an extremely clever manipulator, a sociopathic personality with superior intelligence, but the ethical sensibilities of a criminal.

Ironically, he has also been my greatest teacher. I have learned a lot from my own mistakes, but from Gwil I learned the truth of Jung's oft-repeated contention that what an analyst *is* has more effect than what he *does*.[6] And without Gwil's bad example I might never have known how careful both analysts and patients need to be. It was from him that I learned how dangerous it is not to see the destructiveness in others as well as in oneself, for I cannot deny that, with the naiveté of the very young, I was his willing—even enthusiastic—victim.

---

[5] CW 4, ¶450.

[6] For example, CW 4, ¶447ff; CW 16, ¶198.

When someone is victimized we tend either to condemn the bully or blame the victim for "asking for it," but blame-placing does not do justice to the psychology of the situation. The adult who permits herself to be victimized when there is something she could do to stop it is in thrall to an unconscious God-image. It can happen to anyone who is too naive. Let me tell you how it was for me.

I still remember the first time I set eyes on Gwil. It was one of those moments that circumvent the usual storage procedures and go straight into long-term memory. For instance, almost every American old enough to remember 1963 at all recalls the moment when he learned of John F. Kennedy's assassination. I believe that Kennedy was so charismatic that the psyche responded as if a god had been sacrificed. Certain private events are engraved in memory for similar reasons. On the surface they may seem quite ordinary, but on a deeper level I suspect they signal that an archetype has been touched, whose numinosity may only become apparent later. My first meeting with Gwilym was like that. If I should doubt that some god lay between us, I need only contemplate the vivid memory of his unexpected entry into one of my graduate seminars. After nearly forty years the picture is still like a flash photograph in my mind—his startling black hair and eyes, and wiry body, dense as lead, settling into one of those wooden classroom chairs.

We were a small group, already weeks into the semester, and the invasion of my space offended me. Much later I would have reason to remember that my initial, instinctive reaction was hostile.

That day one of my classmates brought a dream into her case presentation. Gwil jumped into the discussion, questioning the student with great authority, as if he were our teacher or, at the very least, had been part of the group from the beginning. He was trying to find out whether the dream-image of the central character differed in any way from the same person in outer reality.

I found the newcomer's questions irrelevant and his domination of the group annoying. I thought about dreams a lot and was pretty sure their meaning went far beyond literal reality even when they appeared to duplicate it. Gwil thought otherwise. Much later he told me he believed that certain dream images, identical to their outer-world counterparts, should be taken literally. The seeds of that conviction, which I have grown to see as potentially quite dangerous in spite of the grain of truth it contains, were evident at our first meeting.

At the end of the semester I dropped out of school and soon lost track of Gwil. A few years later he popped up again, phoning to ask if I would look at a paper he had written. He must have gone to a lot of trouble to track me down, but it did not occur to me to wonder why he bothered.

The article was brilliant. No doubt about it. It touched one of my own areas of interest, the intersect between spirit and matter, and made some remarkable inferences that would never have occurred to me. One section of the paper fascinated me. An intricate and closely reasoned series of arguments, it revealed a quality of mind I had not seen in Gwil before. My estimate of him began to rise. I called to express my admiration and ask about some points that were not entirely clear. Later that week we met in my small attic apartment and talked for several hours. I have forgotten the details of our conversation, but the peculiar dream I had that night sticks in my mind. It was set in my apartment and at first seemed to duplicate the day's events. In the dream, however, as Gwilym and I sat talking, his penis suddenly entered me. As we continued to converse, we both had orgasms, although we were fully dressed.

And so it was. No respecter of boundaries, Gwil's spirit got into me without waiting for either of us to undress. I felt obscurely flattered, unaware that such a seduction might be less than desirable. It was a deceptively sweet satisfaction, akin to what I would feel during my first years as an analyst whenever a patient dreamed about me. Now I realize that dreams do not pay compliments but are, as Jung suggests, a piece of nature about which it is "up to us to draw conclusions."[7] If we do not draw the right conclusions, there will be consequences. About my dream of Gwilym I came to no conclusions at all.

• • •

Trying to reconstruct the details of those years, I search through appointment books and dream journals that reach back into the 1950s. In view of Jung's contention that each moment in time has its own peculiar quality, creating "a synchronicity between the psychological events in ourselves and the events in the sphere of life in which we live,"[8] the discovery that Stephen Como became my lover less than two weeks after I made Gwil my analyst should not come as a surprise. The psyche's miracles still astonish me however, and I am amazed.

I was not yet aware of a psychological reality that I now take for granted: if the numinous aspect of an analytic relationship is not understood deeply enough, it is likely to be acted out unconsciously in a sexual relationship. Often enough the God-image that is aroused leads to sex between analyst and patient, but sometimes it kindles an attraction to someone entirely different who embodies a similar God-image.

On the face of it Steve, with whom I had a hot and wildly irrational love affair, was not at all like Gwilym. He had grown up in Montreal, graduated from Harvard, and claimed to be a second-generation Russian Jew. The name Como seemed singularly un-Jewish, but he did look like a Jew. He also looked Italian but, in my innocence, I simply accepted what he said, unable to imagine that anyone would misrepresent his identity.

---

[7] CW 15, ¶161.
[8] *Nietzsche's Zarathustra*, vol. I (Princeton: Princeton University Press, 1988), p. 423.

Steve was secretive about what he did for a living, saying only that he was "in business." He always had a lot of money and I was hounded by the fantasy that he trafficked in illegal drugs. In retrospect, only one thing is clear. Stephen Como was not what he appeared to be and neither, if I but had the wit to see it, was my "analyst" Gwilym Rees.

• • •

To say that I made Gwil my analyst is not entirely accurate. For one thing, his training was a little equivocal and there was some question about his right to call himself an analyst. For another, he actually made *himself* my analyst and I went along with it. I asked him dubiously if he thought we could work together, considering that we were peers and sometimes had social contact. The question was hardly formed before he said "Yes!" and took out his appointment book so decisively that my misgivings stuck in my throat. This set the pattern for everything that happened later. Whenever I doubted something Gwilym said, I would feel incomprehensibly blocked, as if some hidden god refused permission to dissent. Gradually I submitted to its subtle domination.

The first thief dream came during the second year of our work, the night after an hour with Gwil:

> *My friend Anna asks me to help apprehend two very dangerous thieves who have turned themselves into flies. She has tricked the flies into coming to my apartment, and has asked the police to come and get them there.*

When I told Gwil the dream, he scratched his head and said nothing. His failure to speak was out of character, for he almost always had a facile intuitive response to some detail of a dream. At the time I had no way to explain his silence, but made a mental note of it because I have something inside—a factor both religious and scientific—that compels me to pay careful attention to my experience. Years later I understood that the dream had touched a complex in Gwil. Then, however, I waited without comprehension.

Finally he asked, "What do *you* think?"

I shrugged. Flies spread infection, I thought. They would be hard to shut out, and nearly impossible to catch. My analyst did not ask about Anna, nor did I volunteer to tell him about her passionate distaste for Gwilym Rees.

"Yech!" she had said to me at dinner the night before. "How do you *stand* the guy? There's something really *creepy* about him."

"How can you say that?" I protested. "He's the most brilliant man I've ever known. And *famous*. God! Barely out of graduate school and he's famous already."

My initial mistrust of him long forgotten, I waxed eloquent about my analyst's mushrooming reputation. After all, I had been the first to see and encourage his outstanding capacities and felt entitled to a kind of reflected glory from the renown that grew by leaps and bounds after Gwilym published the paper that had so impressed me.

Anna was unmoved. Like some Delphic pythoness she muttered into her soup, "It'll end badly. Mark my words."

I mentioned none of this to Gwil, and we soon left the dream for safer ground. That night I dreamed:

To my horror I discover that extremely valuable items, some pure gold, have been stolen from my yard. I have no record of their value and doubt that my insurance will cover the theft. I regret not hiding them better, for they were in plain sight, a clear invitation to thieves.

Once again, Gwilym was uncharacteristically silent when I told him the dream. Several months later, a third thief dream announced that my volumes of Jung's Collected Works had been stolen. Fascinated and stunned by the activated archetype, I failed to ask some crucial questions: What did it mean that my boundaries were so unprotected? Why was my psyche obsessed with thieves?

Thief dreams are not at all unusual, especially during early stages of a depth analysis. We feel robbed when our unexamined assumptions and values are challenged. The alchemists gave the name Mercurius to the thieving spirit, and said that he "has kept the mind of man busy with his deceptive arts and healing gifts."[9] Sometimes depicted as a serpent, Mercurius is an unstable god who can destroy a person unless she is clever enough to trick, contain, and bear his spirit consciously, much as the boy in the fairy tale got the spirit to return to its bottle and Anna hoped to catch the flies in my dream. It is perilous to forget that Mercurius' "main characteristic is duplicity."[10]

The alchemists imagined mercury to be a dangerously ambivalent element which, however, was a necessary catalyst for change. They believed that Mercurius, god of thieves, would show his helpful face to anyone who sincerely sought the truth, but for people with the wrong attitude, the light of nature would turn into a perilous "foolish fire." When that happens, says Jung, the guide to the psyche becomes a "diabolical seducer," and "Lucifer, who could have brought light, becomes the father of lies."[11]

Speaking psychologically, this means that dreams and other unconscious material can bring illumination to anyone willing to swallow the bitter pill of objective self-understanding. But when the authentic desire for truth is lacking, inner work falls into the shadow and mercury's poisonous side prevails.

---

[9] CW 13, ¶239.
[10] CW 13, ¶267.
[11] CW 13, ¶303.

• • •

Had I been more conscious, I might have suspected that my recurring dreams of being robbed hinted that something was wrong. What did it mean that my volumes of Jung were stolen? They contained the very principles upon which my work with Gwilym purported to rest. And what of the gold, the psyche's supreme value? What had become of it? In my unconsciousness, I neither considered these questions myself nor raised them with my analyst.

If the truth be told, I did not ask Gwilym any questions at all. Steve was another matter. Whenever he took one of his frequent business trips to Montreal, I became gripped by the notion that he had a lover there, and besieged him with questions: "Where are you staying? Why aren't you ever in your room when I call the hotel? Are you *sure* there isn't another woman? What about Martha?"

Steve was indignant. He and Martha had grown up together, he said, and had a brief but unsatisfactory love affair years before. She was an old and trusted friend with whom he now sometimes had dinner.

I spent countless hours trying to understand the source of my jealousy, but it persisted. Whenever Steve went to Montreal I suffered agonies, drove him to distraction with compulsive questions, and phoned him repeatedly.

"I *was* in my room Saturday night," he would say. "I was asleep. I told them not to ring me."

"But," I would protest, "they *said* they rang you and you didn't answer."

He would roll his eyes and explain, as if to a very small child, "Janet, they rang the wrong room. I know where I was, and they did NOT RING ME."

God knows, I wanted to believe him, but something in me refused to leave the matter alone and I made a scene every time Stephen went to

Montreal. I kept trying to escape my suffering by leaving the relationship, but every time I did, the eroticism between us intensified and I did not have the strength to give it up. It was as if I were chained to that hellish wheel until I could learn the truth.

Perhaps this is the crux. Many years later I realized that Truth (with a capital T) is my highest value, the gold of which I was robbed in my dream. I feel cheated by polite, culturally-sanctioned substitutes for the psychological reality that can be glimpsed behind the scenes. Truth is so numinous to me that when it is willfully hidden it acts like a magnet, binding me to the most impossible situations until the mystery is uncovered.

I had been with Steve for two long years when a miracle happened. One day I phoned him at the precise instant that he dialed his answering service, and I found myself improbably connected to his conversation. After my first, abortive attempt to be heard, something told me to keep quiet and listen.

Steve was saying, "Martha. Aren't there any messages for Martha Simpson?"

"Oh. Yes, sir," said the answering service person. "There seems to be some interference on the line. Martha has three messages . . . "

It came to me that Martha was now in residence in Steve's apartment. My arteries filled with ice, and I quietly hung up the phone. Later, when I knew Steve would be out, I left a message for Martha under an assumed name. She called back right away and I asked her to meet me for coffee at the corner delicatessen where Steve and I sometimes had lunch.

I got there early and sat where I could watch the door. She was everything I was not: slim, self-confident, impeccably-groomed, street-smart. As she approached the table, her smile held a trace of pity, and I realized with a shock that she already knew what I wanted to talk about. This lady was cool. Our meeting would not be the hairpulling slugfest I had anticipated.

Still, I was reluctant to open the conversation. We made small-talk until her coffee arrived, then she was the one who jumped in.

"Steve's still fucking you, isn't he?"

I swallowed hard and nodded. She went on, "He told me he had stopped. What did he tell you about me?"

My mouth opened and closed a couple of times. Then I laughed. "He said you were just friends."

"The thing is," she said, "I'm afraid I'll get a sexual disease. I think there's someone in Boston, too. My things are on the way here from Montreal, but I told him I wouldn't move in with him until he gave up all his other women. He said he had." After a short silence she went on. "Do you know about the paternity suit?"

I shook my head.

How Steve expected to continue his Captain's Paradise with Martha living in his apartment was beyond me. For some reason, I was beginning to feel better than I had for a long time. Maybe it was because I liked Martha. She was clearly the better woman. She loved Steve without illusion, but now that my illusions were gone I had to face the fact that I did not love him. The truth had set me free.

Well, almost free. Steve had already provided the opportunity for me to see a lot about myself that belied the sweet young thing I thought I was, and the worst was yet to come. To satisfy the fury of a woman scorned, I filled a box with the dung the dogs in my apartment building left in the back yard, wrapped it in pretty paper, addressed it to Steve and left it outside his door with a Hallmark card. To the card's saccharine sentiment I added a handwritten message: "Dear Steve, I want to give you back just a little bit of what you've given me in our years together."

When I told Gwilym, he stepped out of character again. "You'd better be careful, Janet," he said. "Stephen isn't used to being treated that way."

Shocked, I wondered how he could know that. The momentary failure of Gwil's analytic cool was the only direct sign I ever saw of his unconscious identity with Steve.

• • •

I can hardly blame you if what I am going to tell you next strains your credulity. To the extent that I can reconstruct it from memory, however, I will describe what happened as truthfully as I can.

While my affair with Steve was grinding to its painful conclusion, I dreamed that I took a trip to Montreal. When Gwil and I discussed it, we focused on the fact that Steve and Martha were from Montreal. I myself had never been there. A month later I dreamed I went there again, and again a month after that. Altogether I had nine such dreams, spaced about a month apart. By the third or fourth, I was bewildered, convinced that I would not keep dreaming the same dream if I understood its meaning. Then Gwil told me he had been invited to give a series of lectures at McGill University in Montreal.

I felt a stab of envy. I had been doing some writing in our area of mutual interest and lusted after the honor of such an invitation. My files contained folders full of notes on the subject, and partly-written chapters that I hoped would evolve into a book. I was preoccupied with this material and it often came up in my hours with Gwil.

"How long have you known this?" I asked, hoping my voice would not betray my feelings.

He shrugged. "I don't know. A few months."

The next question leapt into my mind. "When I had the first Montreal dream. . . . Did you know it then?"

His brow wrinkled. "I'm not sure. Maybe. I'd have to check the date of the letter."

The dreams continued to recur as regularly as my menstrual period. As a last resort I decided to travel to Montreal, hoping the city's sensory reality would tell me something I did not already know. I was eager to hear Gwil's lectures, so I timed the trip to coincide with them.

I spent my days in Montreal devouring the sights, sounds and smells of the city, searching almost at random for clues to its meaning. In the evenings I went to the lectures. Although they were not up to Gwil's spectacular first paper, they were received enthusiastically and I was proud to be associated with him. Having spent much of my life until then in classrooms, I felt more at home in the lecture hall than in the city streets. I relaxed and let my mind wander, enjoying the familiar ring of the great man's voice and basking in vicarious glory.

Midway through the second lecture a voice within me intruded on my consciousness:

"This is the meaning of your Montreal dreams," it said. "Your work is in these lectures. Gwilym has brought you here through them."

The idea shocked me. I squirmed in my seat and began to listen more carefully. What Gwil was saying was indeed close to my heart, even close to the material in my files at home, but the words were not mine and some of the ideas were far from anything I would have said.

Silently I spoke to the voice in my head: "Don't be ridiculous. Do you imagine he stole the stuff out of my files? Impossible. He would never do a thing like that. Anyway, he has no access to my files."

"Not your files, stupid," said the voice. "Your psyche."

"Oh sure. A vampire." I laughed out loud and a woman in the next row turned and stared. I put my hand on my lips. The voice said no more.

After the lecture I went up to speak to Gwil. Instead of congratulating him, I found myself saying, "Well, I've gotten what I came for. Now I understand those dreams. *You* brought me to Montreal." He gave me a sharp look but did not ask what I meant.

After that there were no more Montreal dreams and I put the incident out of my mind. Neither Gwil nor I mentioned the subject again and, without exactly deciding to, I abandoned my embryonic book. I had silenced the inner voice whose unsettling message was too bizarre to take seriously, but I could not forget it altogether.

• • •

Contemplating these events today, the experienced analyst sees the seeds of psychosis. The patient—I myself—appears to have slipped into a delusional state. Diagnosis: Acute Paranoid Disorder. This accords with my observation over the years that the image of a vampire in dreams or imagination often accompanies paranoid ideas.

Paranoia can be seen as a psychological split that occurs when large parts of the psyche are projected on outer reality. At the time of her visit to Montreal, our patient has worked for three years with an analyst who encourages her to look at many dreams as expressions of outer reality alone, thereby cutting her off from their inner meaning. The longer she works in this way, the more paranoid she becomes, because more and more of her psyche falls into projection. Since her analyst is likely to see his own dreams in the same way, and the patient has become quite identified with him, we might consider an alternative diagnosis: Shared Paranoid Disorder. Perhaps a latent paranoia in him has induced a similar state in her.

The analysis has reached a point described by Jung, when the work "touches the unconscious and establishes the unconscious identity of doctor and patient. . . . This leads . . . to a direct confrontation with the daemonic forces lurking in the darkness. The resultant paradoxical blend of positive and negative, of trust and fear, of hope and doubt, of attraction and repulsion, is . . . the hate and love of the elements, which the alchemists likened to the primeval chaos."[12]

For the patient to suppress the irrational inner voice is no doubt the better part of valor. Otherwise she might go right around the bend. And yet. . . What she has told us attests to the accuracy of her intuition, which led her to the truth about her lover's double life. The boundary between inner and outer reality has become a little blurred, but it is, after all, rarely as clear as we like to think, as Laurens van der Post suggested when he said, "I have never doubted that the physical world is spirit seen from without and the spirit is world viewed from within."[13]

If we conclude merely that our patient is delusional, some questions will be left unanswered. Why, for instance, does her fantasy take the particular form that it does? Specifically, what makes her imagine that her analyst has plagiarized her work? If we stretch Heisenberg's uncertainty principle a bit, it suggests that at this stage scientific scrutiny might distort beyond recognition the thing we want to observe. Perhaps we should veil our piercing diagnostic gaze and let the patient tell the rest of her story.

• • •

When something is numinous it is like a sore tooth. It will not leave you alone and you cannot leave it alone. Even after my work with Gwil came to an abrupt end, I could not stop obsessing about him. I kept turning my memories this way and that, and for several years he was a frequent and not entirely welcome visitor to my dreams. Apparently I had unfinished business with him.

———

[12] CW 16, ¶375.
[13] Laurens van der Post, *Jung & the Story of our Time* (New York: Pantheon Books, 1975).

I did not look directly at the events in Montreal, but they burned in peripheral vision like pyrotechnic catherine wheels. Still, life went on. I moved to another city and the image of the dark young man who had been my analyst began to fade. If it were not for Audrey and the red cape, I might have managed to forget him altogether.

Audrey grew up in the city where Gwil and I met, and was in therapy with him for half a year. Then she moved to London and eventually, as fate would have it, to the Pacific Northwest where she began analysis with me. She spoke of Gwilym rarely, but I sensed a reservation about her work with him. When she finally brought it up, I was all ears.

"For some reason," she said, "I've been thinking about something that happened a long time ago, when I was in therapy with Gwilym Rees. Would it be all right if I told you about it?"

I nodded and she went on. "In London I met a woman who had a marvelous red cape. Something about it really got to me. I wanted one, wanted it more than anything in the world, but there was nothing like it in all the shops in London. Then, when I came back to the States, I happened upon a red cape in a department store."

She took the coveted item into a dressing room and tried it on. Then, suddenly, she stuffed it into her voluminous purse, almost as if in a trance. She was walking out the door when the store detective tapped her on the shoulder.

"Is there something in your bag that you have not paid for?" he asked.

"Yes," she said, and opened the purse. She felt so humiliated by the events that followed—the trip to the police station to be booked, the bench trial, the suspended jail sentence, the fine—that she managed to keep the whole thing a secret from her family and friends.

When I asked if she had ever stolen anything before she shook her head. "No. That's just it. I was completely shocked. I brought it up with Gwilym because I wanted to understand why I would do such a thing.

And do you know what happened? He threw back his head and laughed. When he stopped laughing, he said not to worry, he sometimes did things like that himself. End of discussion."

Audrey and I talked about Little Red Riding Hood, innocent victim of the devouring wolf. With regard to the red cape, my patient's wolfish greed and envy had apparently eaten her alive, in broad daylight. But why did Gwilym take the matter so lightly? And was it a coincidence that Audrey was moved to steal just then, during her few months of work with him?

As I chew on these questions, there is a knock at my inner door. I open it a crack and a voice on the other side says, "Remember? Remember what happened to you?"

It is all I can do not to slam the door shut forever. That night I dream:

I am considering moving into a communal building, with shared kitchen, laundry, and living facilities. Gwilym and some other men are watching television in a room in the basement. Suddenly I realize I don't want to live in this place. Then, in my purse, I find a picture of the building I'm looking for. It is quite different from this one, and is across the street from The Ethics Society.

My parents instilled in me profound respect for personal property and an uncompromising conscience that makes it hard to filch pencils or accommodate the small lies that oil the gears of social intercourse. But in the wake of Audrey's confession, I have to face the fact that when I was seeing Gwilym my standards began to slip, tempting me away from "The Ethics Society" to a place where property boundaries were quite unclear.

Do not misunderstand. I did not steal anything, but I was seized by a cavalier disregard for my former values, as if a thieving spirit I had never before admitted to consciousness rose up and filled me with its ideas. "Go ahead and take the pencil," it would whisper. "What's so bad about that?" Or, "Why do you report all your income to the government? *Everyone* skims something off the top." The voice urged me to bend the rules more and more. A little here. A little there.

Why do I imagine that if I had discussed these matters with Gwil he would have sided with the thief? No sooner do I ask the question than an image of a large electric typewriter floats into consciousness. Some letters and numbers stamped into the metal on the side of the machine draw my inner vision like a magnet.

I cannot deny that I recognize this typewriter. Gwilym loaned it to me one spring, when my portable broke down. I had qualms about accepting it because I never feel quite right about using someone else's things, but the means to keep working on the paper I was writing was too tempting to resist. When the article was finished, I had another assignment. Gwil said he hardly ever used the machine and told me to keep it as long as I liked. I was enormously grateful and did not return it for several months.

I did not let myself know it at the time, but anyone with half an eye could see that the inventory number on the typewriter's side identified it as the property of the university Gwil and I had once attended. Later he proposed that I use his movie camera. Again I hesitated, but could not resist the use of equipment I could not afford to buy. The camera, too, belonged to the university. So did the projector Gwil urged me to borrow when my film was finished. Denying the evidence of my senses, I refused to believe that a man of Gwil's stature could possibly be a thief. To the extent that I thought about it at all, I imagined he had bought these items from the university. I could not afford to think otherwise. If I saw that my analyst was so much less than he appeared to be, I would have to look at my own primitive shadow. In much the same way as Audrey's greed had devoured her, my unexamined covetousness held me in thrall to Gwilym.

• • •

The fairy tale "The Master-Thief" begins when a splendid coach drawn by four black horses arrives at the home of a poor gardener and his wife. The visitor is the couple's ne'er-do-well son who ran away from home and became a thief, but his parents do not recognize him. Because he wears the cultural trappings of success, they believe he is a great man.

The son reveals his identity and brags that he is an "arch thief." His father is afraid that the count who rules the realm will hang the young man, but the thief is also the count's godson, and the count is thrown into conflict. If the young man is truly a *master*-thief the count will spare him, but he must prove it by performing three tasks. First he has to steal the horse from the count's stable; second, the bedsheet from under the count and his wife as well as the wedding ring from her finger; and finally, he must steal the parson and clerk from the church.

The young man is indeed a master-thief, and a shrewd student of human psychology as well. It is most enlightening to study his methods, which are those of the typical con man. Repeatedly disguising himself as someone he is not, he takes advantage of the human frailty, naive emotions, unexamined assumptions, and unconscious expectations of his victims.

The first night, the thief pretends to be a sick old woman. The soldiers guarding the count's stable feel sorry for him and offer him shelter. He returns their kindness by getting them drunk, after which he easily steals the horse. The psychopathic murderer in the film "The Silence of the Lambs" uses the same ploy. Pretending to have a broken arm, he struggles to get some furniture into a panel truck. His intended victim pities him and offers to help. When she is carrying one end of a sofa and he the other, it is easy for him to maneuver her into the truck and close the door. Serial killer Ted Bundy used the same device, feigning injury to trap some of his victims.

On the second night, the master-thief steals the body of a criminal from the gallows and climbs a ladder to the count's bedroom, putting the dead body up ahead of him. The count shoots the body and goes down to the garden to bury it, thinking he has killed the master-thief, who then impersonates the count and enters the dark bedroom. The thief persuades the wife to give him the bedsheet, ostensibly to wrap the body for burial. The wedding ring is a little harder, but she finally gives it to him because she is an obedient wife who cannot say no to her husband.

The third night, the master-thief takes a sack of crabs to the church-yard, puts a lighted candle on the back of each, and lets them run free. Then he dons a monk's cowl and climbs into the pulpit, ranting and shouting that the end of the world is at hand. He says he is St. Peter and offers to take anyone to heaven who climbs into his sack. The terrified clerk and parson oblige and the master-thief locks them in the pigeon-house.

The first page of this story contains a curious excursion, so different in flavor from the rest that I suspect it is a later interpolation. Before the master-thief discloses his identity, he and his father have a philosophical discussion. The old man is planting trees and comments that once a tree has grown crooked it cannot be made straight again. The thief replies, "That is how it was with your son. If you had trained him while he was still young, he would not have run away; now he too must have grown hard and misshapen." Thus does ancient folk wisdom precede the modern psychotherapist's experience that when the twig is bent into a sociopath-ic pattern, the tree is not likely ever to grow straight.

• • •

Once Gwilym, in a chummy mood, told me he came from a family of small-time swindlers and con artists. No doubt it was a measure of my naiveté that I was not put off. Gwil rarely confided about himself, and with hindsight I have puzzled about why he told me that. Did he have some need to warn me about the darkness in his nature? Did he want to puncture my inflated, idealized image of him? Or what? Loaning me his stolen property had a similar quality, as if he were flaunting his transgressions. But the more he dared me to *see*, the harder I was driven to look the other way. How could I doubt the integrity of such a kind and helpful man, especially one so highly respected?

Still, his strange behavior occupied a corner of my mind for years, waiting for a convincing explanation. I did not find one until I saw the movie "The Grifters," a vivid portrayal of the world of the confidence artist. One scene depicts a swindler's excitement at skating on thin ice, defying a victim to see that he is being conned. The more unconscious the prey, the more extreme the gratuitous risks the predator takes, as if innocence heightens his lust for blood. In the scene in question, a con man and his female accomplice play their victim like a fish. While she sits close to the dupe on the couch, flattering and titillating him sexually, her partner offers to show him a room full of non-existent computers, goes right up to the door, even begins to open it. The lady clutches the poor sucker's arm and implies that such an important man should not be bothered with trivial details. With a show of reluctance, the con man closes the door. It is a masterful piece of teamwork, the action moving between them in ever-escalating arousal, to climax in a later scene when the prey is finally taken.

In the darkness of the theater, I felt shock upon shock of recognition. Watching these people take advantage of the human failings of their victims, I became painfully aware that my own ambition, greed, and susceptibility to flattery were what had made it possible for Gwilym to hook and hold me. Then, too, the sparsely-furnished, anonymous rooms in which the grifters lived took me back to the last year with Gwilym, when he invited me to his home and introduced me to his wife Nora. I managed to overlook the household's chaos and its lack of individual aesthetic, but my unconscious was disturbed and I dreamed:

> Gwil's house is a mess. A toilet sits right out in the open and two children are playing on the floor near it. The stink of urine is overpowering. One of the little girls wrinkles her nose and complains about the smell. The other agrees, but they go on playing there anyway.

It is embarrassing to report that I did not get the message. The little girl in me went right on playing in the filth, but somewhere the bad smell had been noted. For the first time I found myself asking questions about some of the things Gwilym said and did. Instead of engaging the issues I raised, he would point in other directions, usually to offenses he said I had committed. Those sessions left me feeling dazed, almost in a state of shock. It took "The Grifters" to help me recognize in Gwil's response the sleight of hand of the confidence artist, who looks his victim straight in the eye while using words to distract him from what the hands are doing.

The last of the thief dreams came two months before I left Gwil:

> I am on a ship crossing the ocean. A man on the ship has done an experiment that I conceived but have not done yet. I know he stole it and published it without giving me credit. I feel angry and helpless.

The dream reminded me of an experiment I had designed for a class in graduate school, the completed work of which I came across several years later, published by my professor in a psychology journal without so much as a footnote to credit me. I did not inquire why this would come up now, so long after the event. I was aware that the image of a ship often refers to the analytic journey, but it did not occur to me that the dream had anything to do with my work with Gwil.

The ensuing weeks are a nightmarish tangle in my mind. I recall that Gwil asked me to be a friend to Nora and I tried to comply, only to be chastised by Gwil when Nora rebuffed my friendly gestures. I remember a moment of terror when Gwil said that his feelings toward me had changed because his 8-year-old son Robert had a bad dream about me. I recall the unexpected surge of fury when my friend Ernie repeated back to me a blow by blow description of my previous analytic hour, which Gwil had reported to Nora and Nora had told Ernie. When I raged at Gwil for violating my confidentiality, he shifted the blame, attacking Ernie for his presumed betrayal of Nora's confidence. I left the session feeling confused and angry.

The last evening was the worst time of all. Gwilym, Nora, and I were in their kitchen drinking coffee, when I felt a sudden blast of cold air, like a solitary gust of wind. I do not recall what I was talking about, but I stopped in mid-sentence and stared at the hot-air register next to my chair. Gwil and Nora were both watching me.

"Did you feel that?" I asked.

"What?" said Nora.

"The wind. There was a cold wind."

Simultaneously they shook their heads. Then, of one accord, they looked at each other and laughed.

A wave of fear engulfed me. *Am I hallucinating?* I thought. *Have I gone mad? Are Gwil and Nora lying? Is this a practical joke?* The ground had dropped from under my feet and I had no idea where to find reality. That night I dreamed:

Gwil and Nora and I are in their kitchen. Under the table is an enormous white rabbit, bleeding profusely from a gash in its side. We try to sew up the wound, but the rabbit dies.

At long last the innocent victim was dead, and I did not return to Gwilym. In the months and years that followed, I struggled to grasp what happened that night. The wind was as palpable as anything I have ever felt. I will probably never know for sure whether or not it was physically real, but I am grateful for it. Without it, I might never have found my way out.

Later I worked with other analysts—good ones—and learned something about myself from each. In a way, though, my solitary effort to piece together the puzzle Gwilym posed has taken me deepest into myself, making him the most valuable of all. Slowly, slowly, over the years I began to suspect that I had fallen victim to a practiced manipulator. The thought was so at odds with Gwilym's public image that I was filled with doubt. I dared not speak of my suspicions, painfully aware that much of my experience during those years lay right at the edge of insanity. Just as Mercurius stands "in the middle between body and spirit," Gwil and I walked on such an edge between inner and outer reality that I could not be certain my perceptions were anything other than fantasies like those of the alchemists, valid in the inner world but nonsense in literal reality.

Then, on a visit to the university where Gwil and I first met, I was blessed with another of those sometime miracles. I wandered into the psychology library and began to browse, opening books at random, reading a little here, a little there. Suddenly the hair on the back of my neck stood up. I had opened an old psychology journal to a section of Gwil's first professional paper, the profound ideas and intricate reasoning of the part I liked best. But the article's author was an obscure psychologist, long forgotten, and the date on the volume was ten years earlier than the fateful day when a man named Gwilym Rees walked into my life.

• • •

That is nearly the end of the story, but not quite. I thought I had gotten to the bottom of the thing and was home free, but as Jung is fond of pointing out, such matters often have a double bottom. If you have not guessed what self-righteous wrath and fantasies of retribution seized me in the wake of my discovery, then you have never been a victim. Much as I would like to leave this package of excrement squarely on the doorstep of Gwilym Rees, I have to give him his due. I needed his duplicitous assistance to give me an inside view of the ugly psychology of the innocent victim, who so easily turns into her destructive, vengeful opposite. The memory of Gwilym keeps me honest, holding me to the elusive, paradoxical, ever-shifting, exasperating Mercurial tension of psyche in transformation and forcing me to see that the nature of psychological Truth (with a capital T) is not so simple as literal, factual reality. "We are told on every side," says Jung, "that evil is evil and that there can be no hesitation in condemning it, but that does not prevent evil from being the most problematical thing in the individual's life and the one which demands the deepest reflection. . . . In the last resort there is no good that cannot produce evil and no evil that cannot produce good."[14]

---

[14] CW 12, ¶36.

chapter four

WALKING WITH
GOOD AND EVIL

The hardest of all lessons to learn in individuation is that one is almost
always holding a tension between opposites. It is so easy, at almost any
point in one's development, to fall into one or the other of the polarities.
—ROBIN ROBERTSON[1]

M y three cats perform a ritual in front of the cat door. Darji grooms her black and white coat to perfection, then approaches the plastic rectangle and hits it sharply with her paw, tapping the door against its frame three times in staccato succession. Next she darts to the left and stares intently out the window. Seconds later she pirouettes and runs to the large window to the right of the door, glances out quickly, then pokes her nose against the cat door, moving it outward in ever widening arcs—tap, tap, tap, tap—after which she sits and looks around. Druid lies four feet behind her. His long brown and white hair spreads out from his enormous body, creating a nearly perfect circle on the floor, and the illusion that movement would be impos-

---

[1] Personal communication.

sible. Thunder, my sleek, gray, old-lady cat, turns away from the scene and begins to wash her face. Only her ears betray that she is aware of every particular of the drama unfolding behind her.

Suddenly Darji shoots through the cat door. Before her hindquarters have disappeared, Druid propels his fat body miraculously across the space and slaps her black and white behind. Thunder moves closer. Her short coat cleansed, she is ready to take her turn at the door.

The dance is repeated several times a day, a theme with variations refined from early feline experience. Whether or not present circumstances warrant such precautions, no cat passes through the door without them.

I marvel at the spontaneous rituals of small four-legged creatures facing the hazards of passage. I am tempted to see in their actions a metaphor for human religious life, but people are more complicated than cats. Our instinct to honor and propitiate unseen powers beyond our control is only part of the picture. Jung put it this way:

> The animal is the most pious thing that exists. It is the one thing except plants that really fulfills its destiny or the superior will— the will of God, if you want to put it into religious language. We are of the devil because we are always deviating, because we are always living something of our own, not fulfilling the divine will. Animals are pious, they live exactly as they were meant to.[2]

Consider the implications: viewed uncritically, my cats are adorable little creatures, but they have no morality. From the point of view of a mouse, say, or the rufous-sided towhee whose mate Darji murdered last week, feline devotion to the natural order of things leaves something to be desired. The consequences of amorality, of just "doing what God

---

[2] *The Visions Seminars, vol. 1* (Zurich: Spring Publications, 1976), p. 40.

says" without bringing conscious ethical principles to bear, can be horrendous.

Animal piety resembles the psychological state of the religious fanatic, who never doubts that God is on his side. Faith in his absolute rightness makes the fanatic feel he is exempt from ordinary ethical standards. Thus, for instance, a cult leader who guides his followers to suicide or murder is usually obeying what he believes to be the will of God. Acting on unexamined instinct, he is as dangerous as an uncaged panther or polar bear.

Gwilym Rees was similarly faithful to the spirit that moved him. He was in thrall to the Godlike power of his predatory instinct and I, as prey, was equally devoted to its authority. Until I left him, neither of us disobeyed or even questioned the thing that gripped us. Our piety was absolute.

It pays to remember that the tone of the word *pious* is not entirely benign. Even its dictionary definition is ambivalent. On the one hand it denotes "having or exhibiting reverence and earnest compliance in the observance of religion; devout." On the other, it means "marked by false devoutness: solemnly hypocritical."[3] We might infer that if a person appears to be wholly pious something is probably hidden, namely, that "devilish" quality Jung refers to, the stubborn insistence some people have on doing things their way, regardless of what God's intentions may be.

Certain myths give form to the paradoxically good and bad quality of this aspect of human nature. In Greek mythology, Prometheus steals fire from the gods and gives it to humanity. Without his heroic thievery, civilized life as we know it could not exist. Nevertheless, Prometheus is severely punished for his crime against the gods. His liver is eaten by an eagle every day and reconstituted every night, a suffering that in some ver-

---

3 *American Heritage Dictionary.*

sions of the myth goes on for the rest of his life. This is an appropriate image for the pain that is part of mature consciousness, which cannot just blindly obey authority, but must take some of the power of God for itself.

In the Judeo-Christian tradition, Adam and Eve commit a crime against the natural order ordained by God when they eat the forbidden apple. Their inability to comply with orders from above, the sinful temptation to think for themselves, is what makes ethical judgment possible, for their illicit meal is the thing that makes them aware of the difference between good and evil. Once they know right from wrong, they can no longer be contained like animals or children in the Garden of the Father God. Forsaking the comfort enjoyed by obedient children, they must endure the discomforts that belong to a conscious adult life.

The alchemists, too, recognized that paradox is intrinsic to the human psyche. Human nature, they said, is *natura contra naturam*—nature against nature—expressing the fact that people have a spiritual instinct that flies in the face of their animal instincts and compels individual development. It is as if we were in contradiction with ourselves from the beginning, and can only become whole by coming to terms with the opposing sides of our nature.

Ten years after Jung's remarks about animal piety and human devilishness, he used psychological rather than religious language to describe the duality of our nature:

> If man were merely a creature that came into being as a result of something already existing unconsciously, he would have no freedom, and there would be no point in consciousness. Psychology must reckon with the fact that . . . man does enjoy a feeling of freedom, which is identical with autonomy of consciousness. However much the ego can be proved to be dependent and preconditioned, it cannot be convinced that it has no freedom. An

absolutely preformed consciousness and a totally dependent ego would be a pointless farce, since everything would proceed just as well or even better unconsciously. The existence of ego consciousness has meaning only if it is free and autonomous. By stating these facts we have, it is true, established an antinomy [contradiction], but we have at the same time given a picture of things as they are. . . . In reality, both are always present: the supremacy of the self and the hybris of consciousness.[4]

It is customary for Jungians to use a capital "S" when referring to Jung's concept of the Self, even though his Collected Works employ a lower-case "s." The capital attests to the transcendent nature of Jung's Self—its relationship to God with a capital "G"—and distinguishes it from the everyday meaning of *self*, as well as the way the word is used by other schools of psychology. Jung's Self concerns the latent wholeness in each individual. He speaks of it paradoxically as both the center and the circumference of the total personality, including both conscious and unconscious aspects. The Self is an archetype that carries the numinosity of the image of God. It is often used as a synonym for the God within.

The ego, as Jung speaks of it, is also different from the ego of other depth psychologies as well as from street usage. I think of my ego simply as the center of consciousness as I know it, my subjective experience of awareness and personal identity.

Jung maintains repeatedly that he does not pretend to know anything about the reality of God. When he refers to God, he says, he means the image of God in the psyche, which at other times he calls the Self. It is necessary to keep this in mind when reading Jung because his language is equivocal and it often sounds as if he were speaking theologically, *i.e.*,

---

[4] CW II, ¶391.

about the objective nature of God. In many contexts I myself prefer the word *God* because, for most people, *Self* is too neutral to do justice to the emotional power of the living experience. Like Jung, when I talk about God, I am almost always, strictly speaking, referring to the image of God in the psyche. I do not know whether there is any correspondence between my image of God and an outer-world transcendent being, but the fact that I mean the God within does not in any way preclude the existence of a God outside the psyche.

Looking at the idea of God in this way is an extension of how I look at many things. It is extremely hard to be certain about the objective nature of anything, because our inner images color our perceptions of outer reality. To know something objectively at all we have to be able to separate it from our own psychology. For example, in the first chapter I mentioned that Oliver Novak's image of his wife Myra initially seemed to have more to do with him than with the reality of Myra. We could say he had a "Myra-image," otherwise known as the anima. While the inner image was not identical to the outer Myra, there were a lot of similarities between them. Otherwise, Oliver would have noticed the discrepancy and given his inner woman a different name.

Similarly, if someone says, "My neck hurts," she may require the services of a chiropractor to correct a physical problem, she may have a psychological "pain in the neck" that is expressing itself in her body, or both. In the event that no physical basis can be found for what she is feeling, we might infer that she has projected a "pain-in-the-neck-image" into literal reality. To complicate matters further, even if the pain does have a physical basis, it may *also* be a metaphor for something psychological, for physical symptoms often prove to be precise symbolic statements about something in a person's psyche. Only by walking a line between literal and symbolic meanings, remaining in the tension between objective and subjective, earthly and spiritual realities, can a person do justice to the extraordinary complexity of psychological truth. Getting stuck on one side or the other creates serious problems. As the writer Virginia Woolf said, "The balance between the outer and the inner is, after all, a terribly precarious business. They depend upon each other with the utmost closeness."[5]

In a dream described by Edinger,[6] the dreamer, a psychotherapist, catches a golden-colored fish and is required to extract its blood and heat it until it reaches a permanently fluid state. The blood is in constant danger of clotting, but keeping it fluid is essential. Edinger discusses the golden fish as an image of Christ. I see the danger of clotting as a symbol of what happens when the fluidity required to stay in the tension of opposites is lost. The consequences are nearly always destructive. For example, the blood of the golden fish clotted for Oliver Novak because his mother and the mental health system were too trapped in the mundane implications of his cross-dressing to understand and support the inner spiritual meaning behind the compulsion. The blood clotted for me when I made the opposite mistake: I projected the inner image of a god on Gwilym Rees, and it blinded me to the concrete reality of who he was and what he was doing. In Oliver's case the inner, symbolic meaning was lost; in mine, it was the literal outer facts.

When I was young I knew a man for whom the blood of the golden fish had clotted for good. He longed for a relationship with God, but was hopelessly imprisoned in the literal. This man—I'll call him Bruce—dreamed repeatedly that he was in a vertical concrete maze, always climbing toward the sky, struggling to find a way out. Years earlier he had quarreled with the priest of his local church. Bruce was convinced that the ritual surrounding the Eucharist had to be done in a very specific way to

[5] Quoted by Rosemary Dinnage in *The New York Review of Books*, May 29, 1997, p. 5.
[6] Edward F. Edinger, *Ego and Archetype* (Baltimore: Penguin, 1973), p. 257.

73

be effective, but the priest, a so-called Low-Church Episcopalian, performed the liturgy with a minimum of ceremonial formality. Enraged, Bruce left the church and never returned, but was unable to develop an individual connection to the deity. He was too stubbornly trapped in his conviction that specific concrete gestures, performed by a duly ordained priest, were the only doorway to God.

Finding no symbolic expression, Bruce's numinous inner images eventually overran his psyche and he lived the last years of his life in a gentle state of dementia.

• • •

It is the beginning of Holy Week, 1997, a few days after the spring equinox. I have just started work on this chapter when the first news reports come in from Rancho Santa Fe, where thirtynine members of the Heaven's Gate cult have succumbed to a carefully ordered, ritualistic group suicide. That weekend, the night sky in the little town where I live is spectacular. The moon goes into nearly total eclipse, the comet Hale-Bopp is dazzling, and Mars hangs huge and red in the space between. It is a numinous moment.

In killing themselves, members of the cult expected to leave their bodies behind and move to a higher state, carried by the spaceship they believed was waiting for them behind the comet. Their leader, Marshall Herff Applewhite, was convinced that he was God or, at the very least, an extraterrestrial representative of the "Kingdom Level above Human."

Spaceships, extraterrestrial beings, UFO's, and other visitors from the sky appear frequently in dreams and fantasies, as well as in films and other vehicles of popular culture. They appear to represent epiphanies, numinous manifestations of the Self, akin to the visions of Old Testament prophets dressed up in contemporary garb.[7] The Heaven's Gate beliefs give form to the psyche's longing for transformation, the urge to "die" to old ways of being in order to be reborn into a "higher" state of consciousness, perhaps a less concrete, literal state of mind.

If Applewhite had grasped the symbolic import of his fantasies, they might have led him to a new and meaningful way of life. The tragedy is that he simply fell under their spell and, in the charismatic state induced when a person is possessed by numinous fantasies, took others with him to their death. Like all fundamentalists, he and his followers interpreted symbolic material literally and acted it out without questioning what they believed God was telling them to do. For Heaven's Gate, the blood of the golden fish clotted with a vengeance, and earthly reality was lost forever.

• • •

In the early 1950s, Jung published an exposition of the Biblical Book of Job that depicted both the difficulty and the crucial importance of sustaining the tension between different realities. *Answer to Job* [8] nearly abandons psychological language altogether to discuss the relationship between ego and Self manifest as an encounter between man (Job) and God. The book is, in part, an outraged protest against God's abusive treatment of his steadfast servant Job. Ultimately, says Jung, God (the Self) was actually changed by Job's (the ego's) capacity to bear the nearly unbearable paradoxes of the deity (the God within). Jung concludes that people are in some sense superior to this paradoxical God, for the latter embodies a part of the psyche that has to be transformed through an

---

[7] See Jung, "Flying Saucers: A Modern Myth of Things Seen in the Skies," CW 10, ¶589–824.
[8] CW 11, ¶553–758.

encounter with human reality. Psychologically, this means that the Self needs our devilish, disobedient, willful ego-consciousness to stand up to it, the very thing that Marshall Herff Applewhite failed to do. Only by confronting the divine imperative can we hope to moderate and humanize its destructiveness.

In view of the fact that human consciousness is divided between the desire to serve the deity and the impulse toward disobedience, it is only logical that the God in whose image we are said to be made would be equally paradoxical. Indeed, an examination of the Old Testament reveals an unreliable and amoral God, imperious, demanding, raging, murderous, predatory, vengeful, and warlike. Torn between conflicting impulses, this God alternately creates and tries to destroy His creation. Such a God-image bears a close resemblance to a part of the human psyche that is so unevolved, even animal-like, that many people either never become aware of it at all or are only able to see it in others. It is mirrored in bloody civil wars around the world today, and apparently random eruptions of violence.

The word *violent* derives from the Indo-European root *wei-*, which means "vital force." Since one definition of the word *God* is "an immanent vital force," we might infer that God and violence are intimately related. Most Indo-European roots have a long list of cognate words but *violent* has only two: *vim* and *violate*, which are opposite to one another in feeling tone. The root *wei-* is thought to be related to another Indo-European root *wiros*, meaning "man." Cognates of *wiros* are also divided between positive attributes like *virility* and *virtue*, and words with negative connotations, notably *werewolf* and *virago*.[9]

Thus, the roots of language suggest that the source of life itself, the vital force that we may think of as God, contains the opposites of good and evil and is fundamentally violent.

---

[9] *American Heritage Dictionary.*

It does not seem likely that we will rid ourselves of the violence in our nature, nor that of the God in whose image we are made. Anger and a wish for vengeance are normal reactions to being wronged, and twenty centuries of admonitions to turn the other cheek have not changed this. As Jung says, "The angry reaction must be stored somewhere if it is not let out openly, and then there is a festering wound; even if the conscious is most Christian and behaves perfectly, that anger is stored somewhere. . . . Any wrong one has received cannot be gotten out of the system unless it is paid by wrong."[10]

Such an extreme statement is hard for the enlightened, humanitarian consciousness to swallow, but no amount of idealism will alter the psychological reality behind what Jung is saying. The unconfronted, untransformed psyche does demand an eye for an eye, and gets its way behind our backs when we fail to face it consciously. Eruptions of uncontrolled violence are inevitable unless we can look squarely at the anger and aggression that are part of human nature and try to come to terms with it in realistic ways. The harm done by violence in the world can only be mitigated by individuals who see, and take responsibility for, the warlike, vengeful, jealous God in themselves and who are also willing to stand up to it in others. If enough people can reach that level of consciousness, perhaps it will become possible to circumvent the most destructive ways in which the vital spirit of humankind is acted out.

During the Third Reich, Hitler and the German people provided horrifying proof of the human spirit's awesome potential for evil, particularly when it is channeled into a mass movement. I believe that Jung's attempt to integrate the opposites at the archetypal center of the psyche forced him to come to terms with the same explosive energies that Hitler acted out. Consider a dream that Jung had in 1939, which he told to

---

10 *Nietzsche's Zarathustra*, vol. 1 (Princeton: Princeton University Press, 1988), pp. 763f.

Esther Harding, who recorded it in her journal. In her words:

> *He found himself in a castle, all the walls and buildings of which were made*
> *of TNT. Hitler came in and was treated as divine. Hitler stood on a mound*
> *as for a review. C. G. [Jung] was placed on a corresponding mound. Then*
> *the parade ground began to fill with buffalo or yak steers which crowded into*
> *the space from one end. The herd was filled with nervous tension and moved*
> *about restlessly. Then he saw that one cow was alone, apparently sick. Hitler*
> *was concerned about this cow and asked C. G. what he thought about it. C.*
> *G. said, "It is obviously very sick." At this point, Cossacks rode in at the back*
> *and began to drive the herd off. He awoke and felt, "It is all right."*[11]

In discussing the dream with Harding, Jung emphasized that Hitler was
not to be seen as a human man but as an instrument of numinous powers, albeit dark ones, "as Judas, or, still better, as the Antichrist must
be."[12]

If Jung said anything about the fact that he, too, was placed on a
mound, his remarks were not quoted. As I see it, the dream shows that
he was up against the same dangerous archetypal forces as Hitler. Both
were placed above the level of ordinary people and treated as divine,
which activated the wild masculine energy symbolized by the buffalo and
yak steers. We know that Hitler was swept away by this dark power. Jung,
on the other hand, was able to confront and integrate it. It is crucial to
understand the difference, for every one of us has Hitler-like energies
inside that can be set in motion under certain circumstances. We need to
realize that the important thing is what we do with this part of our
nature.

---

[11] Wm. Mcguire and R. F. C. Hull (eds), *C. G. Jung Speaking* (Princeton: Princeton University
Press, 1977), p. 181.
[12] *C. G. Jung Speaking*, p. 181.

Hitler's violence and what he did with it is history. Jung's is not so well known. Aniela Jaffé said a little about it in *The Life and Work of C. G. Jung*.[13] When Jaffé became Jung's full-time secretary, in his 81st year, she had already known him for nearly twenty years, first as his analysand, and later as an assistant on some of his projects. These relatively limited contacts "took place in a protected area sealed off against everyday life, forming islands of peace in the flux of time." Now that her association with Jung would be more extensive, he warned her that he sometimes had spectacular outbursts of anger, and told her not to take them personally. He saw that even if another person triggered his violent affect, she was not the source or cause of it and should not be blamed. Jaffé was grateful that Jung took full responsibility for his outbursts. She wrote:

> The old man's honesty, his regard for my sensibilities in warning me of his easily aroused anger and of his tendency to give vent to his annoyance, were an expression of his relatedness, in which consideration and hard driving both played a part. This duality in his nature was perfectly genuine and evoked trust and allegiance. Till then I had known nothing of Jung's violent side.

Today, many people find themselves having to deal with violent affects, forces of superhuman proportions that have traditionally been assigned to Satan or the devil. As fewer and fewer people's spiritual needs are met by the established religions, the power of gods and demons flows into the human psyche and often runs amok, expressing itself in experiences of murderous rage and suicidal self-abnegation, in psychosis and addiction, in the compulsions that force us to act against our best intentions, over and over again.

---

[13] Trans. R. F. C. Hull (New York: Harper/Colophon, 1971), p. 101.

It is sobering to realize the enormous potential for evil consequences when a person is not strong enough to endure an influx of archetypal energy without becoming possessed by it. Hitler may be the 20th century's most shocking example but he is hardly the only one. For instance, any cult leader can easily become identified with God and, in the grip of the dark side of the deity, lead his followers to violence against themselves or others. The last decade of the millennium has brought a veritable epidemic of such incidents. At this writing we have seen David Koresh of the Branch Davidians, Luc Jouret of the Order of the Solar Temple, Shoko Asahara of Aum Shinrikyo, and of course, Marshall Herff Applewhite of Heaven's Gate. In the 1960s, Charles Manson and the Manson "sisters" were harbingers of things to come, followed in the 70s by the Reverend James Jones and the residents of Jonestown. Like all leaders of groups that culminate in mass suicide or mass murder, these people were confident that they were carrying out the will of God.

In contrast stand lone individuals who, like Jung, seek ways to transform the God within, questioning the imperatives that come like messages from above and confronting "what God says" with the reality of human needs, values, and ethical concerns, carrying the tension between ego and Self until solutions acceptable to both emerge from the conflict.

I have the impression that the two mounds in Jung's Hitler dream represent an aspect of the problem of opposites that all Jungian analysts and therapists have inherited and must come to terms with. The kind of work Jungians do can be infinitely creative, but a constructive outcome is not guaranteed. Because they work with numinous material, they are even more likely than other helping professionals to activate God-images in their patients and consequently to be placed on "mounds," elevated to a superior position. Having thus gained inordinate power as a result of transference projections and through no merit of their own, they are under constant pressure to be like Gods. When they succumb to the temptation, the demonic "Hitler" side of the unconscious is as likely to incarnate as the benevolent "Jung" aspect. As a result, patients are sometimes badly exploited, their lives damaged or even destroyed.

From painful personal experience on both sides of the consulting room, I can attest to the fact that this is a significant occupational hazard for Jungian analysts. Understanding the full implications of Jung's Hitler dream can to some extent alleviate the problem.

• • •

Near the end of *Answer to Job*, Jung alludes to the nuclear holocaust the United States had unleashed a few years earlier at Hiroshima and Nagasaki.

> Everything now depends on man: immense power of destruction is given into his hand, and the question is whether he can resist the will to use it, and can temper his will with the spirit of love and wisdom. He will hardly be capable of doing so on his own unaided resources. He needs the help of an "advocate" in heaven . . . who brings the "healing" and making whole of the hitherto fragmentary man. Whatever man's wholeness, or the self, may mean *per se*, empirically it is an image of the goal of life spontaneously produced by the unconscious, irrespective of the wishes and fears of the conscious mind. It stands for the goal of the total man, for the realization of his wholeness and individuality.[14]

How can we reach the goal of totality and realize our wholeness and individuality? This is what Jung called individuation, a process often set in

———

[14] CW 11, ¶745.

motion in the psyche during the second half of life. By examining dreams, fantasies, and other unconscious manifestations, a person can make the process conscious. This permits the conflicting aspects of the psyche to come into awareness and, *Deo concedente* (God willing, as the alchemists were always careful to say), find a way to live together in the individual. Anyone who can carry such a process is in a position to facilitate the birth of a new eon and a new image of God—an era of individual responsibility for good and evil, and a God-image that brings the opposites together into a unified whole.

The words have a glorious ring to them but the reality, when the work is done right, is extremely demanding. It requires a person to face and take responsibility for everything she is, conscious and unconscious, while seeing and differentiating herself from everything she is not. This is painful, grinding, grungy, often depressing and lonely work. At the beginning of it, most of us know ourselves little, if at all, and are enmeshed with all kinds of people and ways of living that do not belong to us. We cling to flattering images of ourselves that honest and objective self-observation calls into question. Few people are able to move far enough beyond the initial state to achieve authentic psychological redemption.

Traditional religions claim that God can redeem us. The alchemists saw it the other way around, that it is our job to redeem God. Viewed psychologically, in terms of the God-image in the psyche, it is both. A unified Self provides the ground for a unified ego, but the help of a more or less intact ego is needed for the Self to become integrated. The paradox must simply be endured. It is not necessary to wait for the gift of wholeness before beginning the work that leads to it, for when the ego sincerely involves itself in its own redemption, the Self comes to meet and wrestle with it. Out of the struggle is born the "heavenly" advocate to which Jung alludes, the helpful transcendent factor in the psyche that makes it possible to go on walking in the nearly nonexistent space between opposites, suffering a virtual crucifixion on the conflicts between ego and Self, good and evil, inner and outer, spirit and nature, human and divine, matter and psyche, real and ideal. This is the individual religious path.

chapter five

THE INDIVIDUAL
RELIGIOUS PATH

*It is not only possible, but fairly probable, even, that psyche and matter are two different
aspects of one and the same thing. The synchronicity phenomena . . . show that the
nonpsychic can behave like the psychic, and vice versa, without there being any causal
connection between them. Our present knowledge does not allow us to do much more than
compare the relation of the psychic to the material world with two cones, whose apices,
meeting in a point without extension—a real zero point—touch and do not touch.*
—C. G. JUNG[1]

"If it doesn't rain, I think I'm going
to die." The sound of my voice
startled me. I looked around to
see if anyone had heard me talking to myself, but no one was paying any
attention. Pam and Gene were fifty feet away on the other side of the
campground, arguing about something, and Kent was behind the car,
changing his clothes. The children were running around looking for wood
for the campfire. Where they got their energy was beyond me. I could only
lie on top of my sleeping bag, stupefied by the relentless California heat.

---

[1] CW 8, ¶418.

Not even the hint of a cloud marred the blazing sapphire sky. I stared at uninterrupted blueness, my mind drifting aimlessly. The sounds and sights of the campground receded and then disappeared. Suddenly a vivid image of native people dancing startled me into consciousness. Energy began to pour into me and I jumped to my feet. "Let's do a rain dance," I shouted. Defying the heat I ignited the campfire and began to circle around the burning sticks, whooping and hollering like a Hollywood Indian. One by one the others joined me until all six of us were yelling and leaping around the fire.

Thirty-one years later even my son Nick, who was only 3 at the time, remembers every improbable detail of what happened next.

We had not been dancing long when a tiny cloud began to take shape in the far distance. Excited by the sight of it we circled faster. The cloud began to move in our direction. It grew larger as it came, fueling our frenzy until we had sung and danced ourselves into a state of near-ecstasy. When the cloud was directly overhead it stopped, opened, and drenched us with the biggest, wettest raindrops I have ever seen. Then, probably no more than five minutes later, the downpour stopped. The cloud dispersed and the sky remained perfectly clear for the rest of our camping trip.

I was stunned. I had entered the ritual naively, expecting nothing. I did not believe that dancing can cause rain, nor do I believe it now. Something in my psyche, however, insists that the two things—rain dance and rain—were not separate, independent events. Against all logic and the laws of cause and effect, something compels me to believe there is a connection between them.

• • •

When there is a statistical correlation between two events, "X" and "Y," it is a common error to assume that "X" has caused "Y" when it is equally likely either that "Y" is the cause of "X" or that a third thing has caused both. For instance, if we are thinking about it causally, we will probably suppose that the rain dance caused rain, but it could equally well be true that a) rain produced the rain dance, or b) something else created both.

In view of the fact that the rain dance came first, the idea that the rain caused it to happen seems absurd. If we take it seriously, however, as a hypothesis, a relatively plausible possibility comes to mind. Let us assume that the atmospheric conditions that created the rainstorm came into being during the time that I was in a virtual trance. Since my intuitive capacities are highly developed, I might well have "smelled" an imminent rainstorm, receiving the information in the form of an image of native people doing a rain dance. My lowered consciousness would have made me exceptionally open to subliminal inputs of the sort that make animals reactive to an approaching storm or earthquake. My impulse to act out the rain dance could have come from a very precise reading, not consciously articulated, of the fact that rain was imminent, as if something in me knew that rain was on the way and was moved to celebrate. Years of self-observation have taught me that my intuition *is* often that exact, so the hypothesis that impending rain created the rain dance is not entirely unreasonable.

A case can also be made for the possibility that a third factor caused both rain dance and rain. Jung has pointed out that when an archetype is activated (or constellated, as Jungians say), it tends to manifest in the physical realm as well as the psychological. Because archetypes have this capacity to jump the gap between psyche and matter, Jung gave them the label "psychoid."[2] In my experience, when an archetype is constellated, it creates a perceptible field of psychological energy, analogous to a magnetic field in the physical sphere. I have long imagined that a field of this

---

[2] See CW 8, ¶420.

sort might "attract" psychological and physical occurrences belonging to a particular pattern, much as a magnet attracts iron filings that make its field visible. As a matter of fact, contemporary mathematicians and physicists seem to be speaking from a similar intuition when they use the word "attractor," describing the fact that a particular motion always settles into a specific pattern; and when chaos theory employs the term "strange attractors" for uniquely individual patterns that are complex and unpredictable, but nonetheless orderly. Looking at the episode of the rain dance from this perspective, we might conjecture that the image in my inner world and the rain in the outer world were both induced by an archetypal field or some other invisible but palpable attractor.

All three hypotheses—that the dance caused rain, that impending rain led to the dance, or that an activated archetype produced both—rely to some extent on cause and effect as an explanatory principle. The problem is that we do not know physical mechanisms that could mediate these particular cause-and-effect relationships. Such mechanisms may eventually be discovered, but current scientific knowledge does not permit these hypotheses to be either proved or disproved.

It is clear, however, that events that appear to be paranormal do occur, even though we do not know how. A number of phenomena that take place in the borderland between conscious and unconscious seem to transcend the boundaries of space and time. For instance, dreams and intuition both behave as if they can perceive events far outside the range of the sensory apparatus, having something like the ability to see through walls and also into the future. Meaningful coincidences of events that are not connected causally also seem indifferent to space and time constraints.

As Jung pointed out, the discoveries of atomic physics show that causality is only approximately (statistically) true. That is, at the microphysical level the laws of causality do not always hold, which suggests that even at the macrophysical level there are likely to be discontinuities.

Indeed, this is the case. In biology, irregularities arise as sports, or freaks. In the psychological realm, says Jung, discontinuity appears in the drive to individuate, which propels a person into a unique individual life often seen as freakish or unnatural. In the physical world discontinuity is expressed in meaningful coincidences, which similarly appear to challenge the natural order.[3]

Discontinuous events are usually thought of as chance occurrences. In many instances this is sufficient explanation. Sometimes, however, we come up against happenings whose coincidence in time does not appear to be random, even though there is no causal relationship between them. Jung felt that modern physics permits—even requires—an additional principle to describe the connection in such cases, and postulated the principle of synchronicity.[4] In synchronistic occurrences the connecting factor is *meaning* rather than causality.

Synchronistic happenings are numinous, perhaps because they seem to defy the laws of nature, or maybe because they bring extreme opposites together. In synchronicity, psyche and matter, spirit and nature, converge. The scientific and religious parts of the psyche meet here, in the encounter between rational understanding and belief. It is as if events of this sort touch a flash point, transforming the stuff of ordinary psychology into the extraordinary material of religion, not the religion of dogma or creed, but the direct experience of the numinous, akin, for instance, to Moses' encounter with God in a burning bush. When synchronistic events begin to happen in your life, or when you begin to notice them, a sense of meaningfulness or purpose often comes unbidden, a feeling of some mysterious intentionality behind the scenes, perhaps even the conviction that you are being led.

---

[3] CW 18, ¶1198.
[4] "Synchronicity: An Acausal Connecting Principle," CW 8, ¶816–997.

• • •

This book grew out of a veritable nexus of synchronistic events. It began as a series of lectures for the 1992 Friends (Quaker) Conference on Religion and Psychology. The conference topic that year was "Meeting the Holy Shadow." When I began to think about what I wanted to say I wondered if accepting the assignment had been a foolish mistake. Talking about the dark side of life had gotten me into trouble in the past, because people did not always discriminate between me and my subject, which gave me more than my share of shadow projections to carry. If I were the main speaker at a conference about the *holy* shadow (a.k.a. the archetypal shadow, Satan, or the devil) I would probably be demonized. Even if I did not tackle Satan head on, he would surely be lurking in the corners.

Someone has to talk about these things, I thought. But does it have to be *me?* My shoulders ached, and I wondered if I would be able to carry the load.

That afternoon I left my writing desk and began my day's work with patients. The first person I saw was a woman in her middle 40s who told me a dream I have come to think of as a picture of The Holy Ghost Descending:

> *It's just a fragment* [she said apologetically]. *An image of a thing made of wood—a mass of gnarled roots coming down at me out of the heavens like a comet. As it gets to eye level, I see perched on it a white, dove-like bird with a white egg between its legs. When the object nears the ground it hovers like a helium balloon.*

Rosalie had been raised a Catholic, but she had left the church and did not think of herself as a religious person. In her analytic work with me, she wrestled conscientiously with the gritty dilemmas of everyday life. At first glance she wanted to dismiss the dream, saying that it was ridiculous and made no sense, but I was riveted. To me, the mass of roots resembled one of those mysterious synchronistic tangles of events that reason says are not connected but, in a manner of speaking, seem to be part of the same great tree. An experience of the holy spirit, pregnant with meaning, can ride into reality on just such a rootball, coming to earth like an asteroid, a flying saucer, or an Old-Testament annunciation angel.

For Rosalie, examining the roots of her psychological problems, following each rootlet to its source, and trying to unravel the meaning of her life was numinous work. This is true for many people today, for whom the individual connection to the numinous to be found in a relationship with the unconscious meets their needs better than the collective religious container provided by church or temple. Unfortunately, most contemporary approaches to psychotherapy, which view the psyche's manifestations as sicknesses to be cured as rapidly as possible, are far from understanding or supporting a religious attitude toward the psychological depths.

Rosalie and I discussed her dream in terms of its meaning for her, but privately I also heard it as a synchronistic message for me, one that helped resolve my conflict about the conference. The dream reminded me that my invitation from the speaker search committee had, in a manner of speaking, ridden in on a tangle of startling and fateful-seeming events that struck the chord of individual identity, making me feel exactly as if my name were being called. Some invitations can be refused with impunity, but to turn away from a piece of personal destiny, the pattern that gives meaning to one's life, is always a mistake. In addition to Rosalie's dream, my rootball consisted of some unusual dreams of my own, a letter that reached me against improbable odds, and many synchronistic connections between me and the conference. I found I had indirect links with the Quakers going back for generations, and even with the woman who originally founded the conference. Then there was the fact that my not yet published book *Saturday's Child: Encounters with the Dark Gods*[5] explored portions of that year's conference theme, the demonic side of deity. Furthermore, I learned that several of the people I had mentioned in the book had specific links to the Friend's Conference. Finally, I had struggled for years to understand and integrate the wild, emotional, instinctual parts of myself. For me, the light was just dawning on the fact that the dark side of the God-image, the conference's "holy shadow," is a mirror for the primordial aspects of human nature living in the depths of all of us.

Each of these connections formed a strand of a rootball like the one in Rosalie's dream, carrying a message from "above," that is, from the realm of the collective unconscious or archetypal psyche. When I paid careful attention to them, I had no doubt that the task of speaking at the conference that year belonged to me and to no one else.

I have already alluded to the fact that the unconscious follows different rules from those of consciousness. In the unconscious, past, present and future events, inner and outer ones, and those occurring in different parts of the universe are mixed indiscriminately together. This makes it extraordinarily difficult to unravel "messages from above," and nearly impossible to talk about them in the linear language of consciousness. For instance, I cannot say exactly when this rootball began, for it has elements that go back at least to the 17th century, but it only started growing in my mind in 1988, when I received a letter addressed to Janet O. Dallett, Seal Harbor, Washington (no zip). The letter was quite a surprise, because in the world of ordinary reality, Seal Harbor, Washington does not exist. It is a fictional place-name used in my first book[6] to protect my privacy. I answered the letter carefully, feeling that it must have more than ordinary significance to reach me in never-never land. Besides, it began with

---

[5] Toronto: Inner City Books, 1991.
[6] *When the Spirits Come Back* (Toronto: Inner City Books, 1988).

the words: "I don't know why I'm writing you except that I have to, the same way I had to read your book," and something numinous nearly always lies behind compulsion.

My correspondence with the writer of that letter led, two years later, to a workshop based on some chapters of *Saturday's Child*, which was not yet published. Soon after that, an unprepossessing, handwritten note appeared in my mailbox asking if the speaker search committee for the Friends Conference on Religion and Psychology might borrow tapes of the workshop. The letter, postmarked Washington, DC, had an extraordinary effect. My heart pounded as if my very blood were crying out, "Pay attention! This is important to you." Perhaps it was the genes of my Quaker grandfather speaking, or the great great grandfather who gave him his name: Tristram Coggeshall, who came to America seeking religious freedom, and who, ironically, was banished from the Massachusetts Bay Colony for defending Anne Hutchinson's belief in salvation through personal intuition of God's grace, dissenting from conventional authority's assertion that salvation had to be earned by good works. My reaction to the letter could also have had roots in something less mysterious than the blood of my ancestors, for I had fond memories of a Quaker college professor who had been kind to me more than forty years before, and I had spent a remarkable summer then with the American Friend's Service Committee, working in Chicago's abysmal slums. The only thing I knew for sure was that I was far more affected than I usually am by the prospect of an invitation to speak. My unconscious was activated and a few nights later I had a dream:

I am traveling, and come to a wild and rocky peninsula I want to explore. I get out of the car and walk toward the end of the peninsula, which appears to be several miles away. Suddenly I catch a glimpse of a long, low, sweeping bridge at the far end, leading to a city that looks like Washington DC. I'm amazed and excited. I can't see much from where I am, but I suspect that once I round the next curve, I'll be able to see the bridge and the city clearly. It takes a while to get there, but when I do, there is indeed a clear view. The bridge is magnificent and the city is Washington D.C. It is much closer than I realized. In another half hour I will probably reach the bridge.

Prepublication copies of *Saturday's Child* came in the mail the next day, a month early. Their unexpected arrival, along with the dream, punctuated my fateful feeling about the letter from Washington DC and gave me an eerie sense of certainty as if, in the unconscious, I had already been chosen to speak. I felt confident that the search committee would eventually come to this conclusion.

In the dream, the bridge was just half an *hour* away. In reality, the invitation came exactly half a *year* later. During this time I searched for the bridge, watching for any links there might be between the rocky peninsula of my dream and the Quaker community on the east coast.

In the outside world, I live on the wild and stormy Olympic Peninsula, a place that convincingly embodies the raw, primordial depths of the psyche that are a source of living religious experience. In story and myth, gods and demons are often said to dwell in such places. In fact the name "Olympic" refers to Mt. Olympus, home of the Greek gods.

In inner reality, my life in that remote spot has put me in touch with awesome and terrible, ecstatic and violent facets of the human psyche that resemble our darkest and most overwhelming images of God. Wotan is one name for the unpredictable and often savage energy of nature untamed. Dionysus and Mercurius are others. Although the Old Testament Yahweh is a later development, He, too, contains a vast reservoir of untransformed primal stuff analogous to the raw power of nature in the outside world and intense emotional reactions in the inner.

If the raw primordial psyche lay at one end of the bridge in my dream, what was at the other? Washington DC is the governing center of a patriarchal culture whose monuments symbolize the highest achievements of a democracy rooted in religious freedom. The city represents a developed civilization whose ideals favor the dispassionate voice of reason, in sharp contrast to the wild-eyed frenzies of Wotan or Yahweh. To the casual visitor at that time, DC appeared to be a pulled-together city. Only the disquieting comments of ubiquitous street people pointed to the irrepressible presence of the primitive shadow.

How can we possibly bridge these extreme opposites in human nature? Jung was deeply concerned with this question. In 1921 he wrote:

> It is . . . impossible to go directly on from our cultural state of today if we do not receive increments of strength from our primitive roots. These latter, however, we receive only if in a certain sense we go back behind our present stage of culture to give the suppressed primitive in us an opportunity to develop itself. How that is to happen is a question . . . with the solution of which I have been occupied for years. . . . In part we need new foundations. Therefore we must dig down to the primitive, and *only from the conflict between civilized man and the . . . barbarian will there come what we need: a new experience of God.*[7]

To become conscious of this level of conflict and carry it requires certain psychological characteristics. The alchemists spoke of the need for patience, courage, perseverance, and a religious attitude, and the avoidance of haste, despair, and deception.[8] In my experience, a firm ground in ordinary reality is also necessary, along with the capacity to wrestle with subtle ethical issues and to look at things as they are, without illusions or sentimentality.

---

[7] Letter to Oskar Schmitz in *Psychological Perspectives*, spring, 1975, p. 81. Italics mine.
[8] Edward F. Edinger, *Anatomy of the Psyche* (La Salle, IL: Open Court Publishing Co., 1985), pp. 5–6.

For many years I myself clung to illusions to such an extent that a colleague commented upon my "malignant innocence."[9] Malignant innocence is a Red Riding Hood kind of naiveté that denies the reality of evil so totally that it does not set necessary limits. Unconsciousness of the human shadow actually invites and encourages exploitation, abuse, and violence from people who will not or cannot limit themselves. Even though I understood that individuals who are unaware of their own shadow are dangerous to others, it took my experience with Gwilym Rees to destroy my malignant innocence and teach me that people who do not see the dark side of others are a danger to themselves.

The image of a bridge between a wild peninsula and Washington DC illustrates the multi-leveled nature of psychological symbols. When you understand a dream correctly, its various meanings will not conflict with one another, but each will deepen the picture like the layers of paint on a work of art. If we look at the most concrete level of my dream, we could say that the image of a bridge was "caused" by a letter traveling from Washington DC to the Olympic Peninsula, as if something in my psyche said, "Aha! That letter is a bridge!" However, the literal connection between me and The Friends Conference rests on something more psychological, namely, my personal struggle to make a bridge between the wild side of my nature and the part that is civilized and rational. To this extent my inner work is part of something larger. It partakes of the problem of opposites in the collective psyche, which must bridge the gap between the light, Christlike side of Deity and its dark, Satanic aspect. We are all participants in that development whether we like it or not, and can either elect to help it consciously or be dragged along with it kicking and screaming, perhaps even to be sacrificed on the altar of a new religious perspective.

---

[9] I am indebted to James Yandell for this expression.

In his book *The Dream: The Vision of the Night*,[10] Max Zeller writes of a dream that he told Jung:

> *A temple of vast dimensions was being built. As far as I could see ahead, behind, right and left there were incredible numbers of people building on gigantic pillars. I, too, was building on a pillar. The whole process was in its first beginnings, but the foundation was already there, the rest of the building was starting to go up, and I and many others were working on it.*

Native people would call this a big dream, one that has import for the whole tribe, not only the dreamer. Jung's comment about it was, "Ja, you know, that is the temple we all build on. We don't know the people because they build in India and China and Russia and all over the world. That is the new religion."

The description of historical changes in the Western God-image in two books Jung wrote late in his life, *Answer to Job*[11] and *Aion*,[12] gives an inkling of what he meant by "the new religion." To summarize: In the beginning, Yahweh displaced the ancient nature gods and goddesses, but some of their qualities lived on in Him. Later God's dark side, in the form of Satan, tempted Him to perpetrate great injustices on a righteous man. These are recorded in the Book of Job. However, Job's growing awareness of Yahweh's unreliable character served to make God more conscious, and once the Deity saw His own abysmal darkness He began to change. He incarnated in Christ in order to transform Himself, but that was just the beginning. Today, says Jung, the incarnation wants to take place in many people through the process of individuation. In this way the highest and lowest aspects of the psyche can come to con-

---

[10] Edited by Janet Dallett (Boston: Sigo Press, 1990), pp. 2–3.
[11] CW 11, ¶553–758.
[12] CW 9–II.

sciousness and be humanized. This means that we have to assimilate forces within us whose contradictions are as extreme as the opposites of Christ and Satan.

In 1956, Jung took up these ideas in a letter to Elined Kotschnig, the woman who founded the Friend's Conference on Religion and Psychology at the nadir of World War II. As fate would have it, I met Mrs. Kotschnig at a workshop in California in 1969. I was 36 years old, newly enrolled in an analyst training program, and dreadfully self-important. She was quiet, unassuming, and 75 years old, the same age as my mother, with whom I did not have a good relationship.

I knew nothing of Kotschnig's connection to the Friends Conference because I did not bother to learn anything about her. In fact, I dismissed her out of hand, but for some reason I did not forget her. The fact that she stayed in my memory for twenty-three years has both a rational explanation and one that is not so rational, making a bridge between two parts of the psyche just as the corpus callosum connects the right and left hemispheres of the brain. Scientific, cause-and-effect reasoning suggests that the name Elined Kotschnig is too unusual to forget. The explanation from the wild side of the psyche is more complicated. There, in the realm of the living spirit, I learn the meaning of my encounter with this woman and its value in the context of my life. Elined Kotschnig got under my skin and touched me in spite of myself. She was numinous to me, and I imagine I discounted her in self defense, because I was afraid she might eclipse or overwhelm me.

A few years later, when Jung's letters were published,[13] it did not escape me that the great man wrote four important letters to the woman who, in my arrogance, I could not be bothered to give the time of day. This gnawed at me. I had the unpleasant suspicion that I had made a

---

[13] Gerhard Adler and Aniela Jaffé, eds. *C. G. Jung Letters* (Princeton: Princeton University Press, 1973). Two volumes.

serious mistake, for I imagined it would take a remarkable person to constellate the things Jung wrote to Kotschnig. When the first of his letters to her was written, I was a babe in arms. The last, dated nine months before I began my Jungian analysis, is, in the words of Edward Edinger, "a wondrous gem, perhaps the most explicit description we have of Jung's vision of the evolving God-image and the human ego's relation to it."[14]

This letter was not consciously in my mind when I wrote *Saturday's Child*, but there are many underlying links between the letter and the raw material of the book. In fact when I began to think about it, a virtual bridge of synchronistic connections between *Saturday's Child* and The Friends Conference came to light. In the book I mentioned three of the Jungian analysts who have accompanied parts of my inner journey. Of the first I wrote, "When a man I cared more about than anyone in the world died suddenly of a coronary, before he had a chance to turn fifty, grief brought me up against the inevitable question: If there were a God, or anything in the universe with more power than I, why would such a good person be allowed to die so young?"[15] I was referring to Jim Whitney, who spoke at The Friends Conference in 1965, the year before his death. His topic concerned the civil-rights movement of the 1960s seen as a metaphor for the problem of integrating the light and dark sides of the psyche.

The second of my analysts named in the book is Max Zeller who, it happens, organized and led the workshop where I met Elined Kotschnig. The third is Edward Edinger, with whom I was in analysis when I began to write about Jung's letter to Kotschnig. During one of my sessions with

---

[14] Tapes of "The New God-Image," seminar given at the C. G. Jung Institute, Los Angeles, 1991–1992. A version of the seminar edited by Dianne D. Cordic and Charles Yates, was later published as a book: *The New God-Image: A Study of Jung's Key Letters Concerning the Evolution of the Western God-Image* (Wilmette, IL: Chiron Publications, 1996).

[15] *Saturday's Child*, p. 14.

him, I mentioned that I was writing about this letter, and he told me that he planned to discuss the same material in a seminar he would be giving later that year.

I was stunned. I did not want to be in the position of competing, or appearing to compete, with someone of Edinger's stature. Like many women, my instinct is to defer to men, especially a man who carries as much of a god-image as Edinger did for me. It felt dangerous to go on with my project. At the archetypal level of the psyche it was as if I had appropriated property that belonged to a god and, like Prometheus or the original parents, I would be punished for my thievery. To add to the problem, on the level of ordinary reality I was particularly sensitive to proprietary rights in the realm of ideas, because on more than one occasion my work had been plagiarized.

When I discussed my dilemma with Edinger he responded with exquisite graciousness. "Be my guest," he said, and as soon as he had presented his lecture he provided me with a tape[16] of the material. For all practical purposes, his generosity allowed me to stand on his shoulders.

• • •

I did not know it at the time, but Elined Kotschnig died in 1983, the same year that I moved to the Olympic Peninsula following a period of great personal and professional upheaval. In the rational realm of cause and effect, there is no possible connection between my move and Elined's death. However, Jung observed something that amounts to a corollary to the principle of synchronicity, that every moment in time has its own unique qualities,[17] lending a similar meaning to events that occur in the

---

[16] Tapes of "The New God-Image."
[17] *Nietzsche's Zarathustra*, seminar notes, James L. Jarrett, ed. , vol. I(Princeton: Princeton University Press, 1988), p. 75.

same time period. For instance, an oracle, such as the I Ching, rests on the assumption that the fall of the coins is connected to everything else going on at the same moment. Similarly, although I do not believe that planets control human lives, an astrological horoscope can be seen as the visible form of a pattern latent in the universe at the time of a person's birth.

When I begin to look into the matter I become aware that quite a few important moments in Kotschnig's life, including the dates of the letters Jung wrote her, coincide with crucial times in my life, particularly major steps in my development as a Jungian analyst. Is this a coincidence, I wonder, or is there more meaning in it than meets the eye?

• • •

In a dream, I try to explain the concept of synchronicity to a colleague, someone who, in the outside world, I think of as having trouble seeing beyond the personal to a larger view of things. This figure is a picture of a shadow side of myself, the part of me that cannot quite get myself around the largest implications of Jung's work, so the dream alludes to the fact that I am trying hard to explain synchronicity to myself. The dream:

> *An image comes to me and I say, "A leaf drops off a tree and falls slowly to the ground, where it eventually ends. That's a life. A second leaf falls and lands where it partly overlaps the first. That's another life. If the area of overlap between the two makes a beautiful pattern, that's synchronicity: It's the third thing, the thing that lies between. If you can understand the pattern, it will tell you something about the relationship between the two lives."*

The connections of which I have spoken describe one of those beautiful patterns. The meaning I experience in the overlap between Elined

Kotschnig's life and mine is what gives me the courage to take up Jung's extraordinary letter to her about the not-yet-transformed God, approaching it as carefully as I would if it had been addressed to me, and scrutinizing each paragraph with religious attention.

chapter six

THE
NOT-YET-TRANSFORMED
GOD

We has met the enemy, and it is us.
—WALT KELLY[1]

J ung's 1956 letter to Elined Kotschnig[2] goes straight to the heart of his most far-reaching ideas. According to a footnote, Kotschnig had asked him "for an answer to the problem of an unconscious, ignorant, creator God," and inquired whether something else might not lie beyond. This is not exactly a common preoccupation and I cannot help wondering what prompted the question. The first American edition of *Answer to Job* was published earlier that year, and I speculate that Kotschnig may have read it and had strong reactions to Jung's outpouring against the God who abused Job. If

---

[1] *Pogo.*
[2] Gerhard Adler and Aniela Jaffé, eds. *C. G. Jung Letters*, vol. 2 (Princeton: Princeton University Press, 1973), pp. 312–316. The letter is reprinted in full in the appendix.

so, she was in good company. The book shocked a lot of people. In fact, as Edinger puts it:

> As soon as you begin to look honestly into the material in [*Answer to Job*] you realize that it's going to offend almost everybody. And if you're not offended, you probably don't understand what he's saying. Either one will be offended that Jung contradicts the familiar God-image that one cherishes in one's own [religion], or if one is a secular rationalist he will be offended that Jung takes so seriously the primitive anthropomorphic God-image that rationalists have long since discredited. One or the other standpoint is going to be offended and it's quite possible that a single person will be offended at both levels at the same time.[3]

Perhaps Kotschnig was offended. In any case, her query evoked an extraordinary response from Jung. I find it hard to imagine how it would feel to find something like it in my mailbox. The content is formidable. Trying to understand exactly what it means brought me up against intellectual and emotional limits in myself that I had never met before. When, after months of mind-bending work, I felt I had more or less fathomed Jung's meaning and began to write about it, I encountered the same barriers to understanding in other people. It is as if the gap between the usual ways of looking at religious concepts and what Jung is saying in this letter is almost too great to encompass. Nevertheless, having gone so far already, I went on wrestling with the material.

Jung begins by telling us how to look at his statements about God:

---

[3] Edward F. Edinger, *Transformation of the God-Image* (Toronto: Inner City Books, 1992), pp. 23–24.

You know that we human beings are unable to explain anything that happens without or within ourselves otherwise than through the use of the intellectual means at our disposal. We always have to use mental elements similar to the facts we believe we have observed. Thus, when we try to explain how God has created His world or how He behaves toward the world, the analogy we use is the way in which our creative spirit produces and behaves.

That is, our ideas about God reflect our own psychology. He is not talking about personal psychology, which is different for each individual, but about human psychology in general. We cannot say anything about God without saying something about ourselves. For instance, stories about how God created the world mirror certain aspects of human creativity.

It is a basic postulate of Jungian psychology that myths and religious stories are projections of material from the collective unconscious, a.k.a. the archetypal psyche, the part of ourselves that all human beings have in common. As I mentioned in a previous chapter, Jung's intentions are not theological. Even though his choice of words does not always make this clear, he is not trying to say anything about the objective nature of God, only about what our images and ideas about God reveal about the human psyche.

It is also true, incidentally, that we cannot talk about other *people* without saying something about ourselves. Whenever I say or think something about someone else, whether it is negative or positive, I take it for granted that it *also* belongs to me and try to see where it is located in my own psychology. It may refer to something I would never *do*, but if I look hard enough I can usually find the thing at least in my feelings. The other person may be living it on an entirely different level or in a different area of functioning than I do, which makes it especially hard to recognize in myself.

Objective self-observation of this sort is not easy. People are capable of an astonishing degree of self-deception and distortion of reality in the interest of preserving a flattering self-image, or even an image that is not so nice if it is comfortably familiar. No matter how hard we try, we can never stand completely outside ourselves. In order to see unconscious parts of ourselves we have to use a mirror. The way our friends and enemies see us, the observations of an analyst or therapist, and our dreams can all function as mirrors for someone who knows how to use them. On the personal level, the things we hate or adore in other people are particularly good mirrors, as are myths and religious stories on the universal human level.

It is easier to see the psyche objectively by looking first at its reflection outside ourselves, then trying to understand how it manifests in our own psychology. So it is that Jung, immediately after telling us that he is talking about the psyche, proceeds to make what sound like statements about God. We have to keep reminding ourselves that he means the *image* of God as it is mirrored in Biblical and other sacred writings.

In the next few sentences of the letter, Jung asserts that if we look at the way the creation has developed, we have to conclude that the consciousness of the creator is limited at best:

> Such a consciousness would necessarily produce any amount of errors and impasses with the most cruel consequences, disease, mutilation, and horrible fights, i.e., just the thing that has happened and is still happening throughout all realms of life.

It is not hard to find outer-world examples of things that make us wonder why, if the Creator knew what He was doing, He did not arrange things differently. One of my favorites has to do with psychological differences between men and women. In view of the fact that the survival of the species depends on a certain amount of harmony between the sexes, why did God make it so hard for us to understand each other?

Edinger points out that the idea of a *dimly* conscious God resolves the conflict between evolutionist and creationist theories of the origin of the species, creationists believing that God intentionally created the world in the way the Bible says, and evolutionists thinking that life evolved through natural selection without any intention at all.[4] Jung's image implies that there is purpose behind creation, but the purposeful agent is nearly blind, and can only realize itself with the help of human consciousness. If we attribute omniscience to such a being, we had better remember, as Jung put it in *Answer to Job*, that God keeps forgetting to consult His omniscience.

What does such a God-image reveal about the psyche? It suggests that there is something unconscious *in us* that wants to realize itself, but can only reach its goal with our conscious participation. For the artist it is a familiar experience to nurture something inside that appears to be groping toward a nearly-invisible goal, emerging as a work of art after a great deal of trial and error. Individuation is a similar process. It could be described as the purposeful but barely conscious movements of the Self, the God within, toward its own fulfillment, taking us up innumerable blind alleys along the way.

At the end of his first paragraph, Jung presents a logical defense of the heretical idea that God is unconscious. If there is nothing outside God, He cannot be conscious because consciousness depends on discrimination. We have no Archimedean point from which to look at something with which we are identical and therefore cannot have objective knowledge of it. In human psychology this means that we cannot know the reality of the outside world, including other people, until we can differentiate ourselves from them. Similarly, if we want to know ourselves, we have to be able to

---

[4] Unless otherwise specified, citations of Edinger's throughout this chapter refer to tapes of "The New God-Image."

step back from transitory inner states in order to look at them. For instance, as long as we have no distance from an emotion we will merely act on it; but if we can disidentify from the emotion enough to stand aside and observe it, it can teach us something about ourselves.

In paragraph 2, Jung refers to the fact that the moral, purposeful, monotheistic God-image of the Jews did not spring up out of nowhere, but grew out of a background of nature spirits and polytheism, much as the Christian God-image developed from the Jewish image. Qualities of the old primitive gods clung to Yahweh, making the personal relationship that he demanded of his followers incredibly difficult. Like the humans said to be created in His image, Yahweh was split. He had wild, primordial characteristics and also more civilized traits. The paradox is expressed by the idea that God is sometimes just and sometimes unjust, an unreliability that has terrible consequences for his followers. In response to this intolerable situation, Jewish prophecy gradually generated an advocate to mediate between God and humankind, a figure that came to be known as the Son of Man.

In the apocryphal Book of Enoch, the Son of Man is described as righteous.[5] This, says Jung, is no accident, for righteousness is exactly what Yahweh lacks, as His treatment of Job demonstrates. The collective psyche, operating as the unconscious often does to produce exactly what is missing from consciousness, created a righteous advocate to compensate for Yahweh's lawless and amoral nature. It is shocking to realize that, according to the sacred writings, we have to have an advocate to protect us from the dark side of God.

What does such a God-image tell us about human psychology? Anyone who has experienced the power of drug or alcohol addiction, overwhelming rage, the impulse to commit suicide, compulsive lust, or

---

[5] Quoted by Edinger in tapes of "The New God-Image."

repeated accidents can attest to the fact that we have within us something that seeks our destruction. The surprising thing is that the destructive factor is intimately related to the same dimly conscious purposefulness that gropes toward the light of consciousness and individual wholeness. Indeed, the instinct to individuate often appears first in a negative form: life-threatening illness, severe depression, an extramarital affair, a psychotic episode. Events of this sort can bring out the worst and the best in us. Whether they will ultimately yield up the treasure buried in such happenings depends in part upon a person's capacity to wrestle with them in a responsible way. As I learned from my experience with Gwilym Rees, the urge to individuate can degenerate into lawlessness and immorality when it is not confronted with human caring and ethical values. In the worst case, this can lead to an individual's total destruction.

The second paragraph of Jung's letter ends with a startling point about the Judeo-Christian God-image, an idea that is extremely difficult to grasp. He says that Yahweh's encounter with Job made God aware of His own destructiveness and motivated Him to improve Himself. However, a change of that sort is not possible without human suffering. In order to become a moral and loving father, God had first to incarnate as a human being, then to sacrifice Himself. In other words, by means of the agonizing transformation process provided by the crucifixion, the destructive God-energy tried to transform itself.

What are the implications for us? It suggests that we can transform the stormy, destructive aspects of our Godlike feelings by suffering them consciously, without either denying them or acting them out. In this way our *unconscious* Godalmightiness can be humanized while our consciousness becomes responsibly Godlike. Edinger puts it this way: "The ego and the Self make overtures to each other, the end result of which is the transformation of God through a double process of the humanizing of the Self and the deifying of the ego."

So, Jung continues in paragraph 3, in *this* world at least, God incarnated and sacrificed himself. To the extent that He succeeded in transforming Himself we know that He is good and that we, too, are good. However, there is a fly in the ointment, for "we don't know how much of God has been transformed. It can be expected that we are going to contact spheres of a not-yet-transformed God when our consciousness begins to extend into the unconscious."

Jung seems to be suggesting that the crucifixion did not change the God in the psyche everywhere and for all time. The evidence lies in pockets of untransformed God-energy that we come across whenever consciousness reaches into the unconscious. It happens regularly in depth analysis, but the contemporary world offers many other ways to enter the unconscious, and people often do it naively, without any knowledge of the maelstrom that can be touched. Countless individuals have unwittingly stumbled into the wild, demanding, stormy side of the psyche without tools for dealing with it. In *Saturday's Child* I describe this part of ourselves as:

> . . . a Power that will stop at nothing to satisfy itself . . . something inside that resembles a tyrannical infant, expressing itself in an unconscious demand for people and events to conform to our insatiable expectations. This part of the psyche is as wild as an animal or the power locked up in the nucleus of the atom. Although it is no more intrinsically malevolent than a blizzard or an earthquake, as long as it is unconscious it can wreak incredible destruction.[6]

Edinger speaks of this energy as the unconscious Self, which can be observed in infants, psychotics, criminals, religious fanatics, and any one of us when we are possessed by a strong emotion. This part of human nature

---

[6] p. 116.

feels entitled to have anything it wants. When its wishes are thwarted, it fills people with self-righteous rage and causes them to run roughshod over the rights of others, sometimes even to the point of murder.

In the United States, the last decade of the 20th century has brought plenty of opportunities to witness the dark side of the God in the psyche, in acts like the bombing of the federal building in Oklahoma City, or the mailing of explosives by the Unibomber. It is hardly ever recognized that events like these are mirrors for something that lives in all of us. We prefer to project such unpleasant human potentials on people as far away and as different from ourselves as possible. Thus, for instance, it was widely and mistakenly assumed at first that foreign terrorists were responsible for the bombing of the federal building and also for the explosion of Flight 800, en route from New York to Paris.

I sometimes suspect that people who are driven to commit destructive acts may be propelled, in part, by the unconscious violence in the psyches of the self-righteous. *I.e.,* if larger numbers of responsible citizens were aware of the violence within them, fewer criminals would perpetrate violent crimes. I hasten to add that I do not believe that criminals should be let off the hook for what they do, only that there would be fewer crimes to punish if we all took responsibility for our share of divine destructiveness.

When the dark side of the God within is repressed or ignored, it often turns into passive-aggressive martyrdom and self-denial, a doormat syndrome that is likely sooner or later to turn into its opposite and step on someone else. The two manifestations of the God-image in the unconscious embodied by the persecutor and the victim are linked psychologically to a third, the rescuer. Taken together, the three form what has been called the rescue triangle.[7] The power-motivated compulsion to

---

7 Claude Steiner, "The Rescue Triangle." Photocopied paper, privately circulated. Also mentioned by Stephen Karpman in "Fairy Tales and Script Drama Analysis," in *Transactional Analysis Bulletin*, 7:39–43, April, 1968.

rescue other people by taking care of their problems, whether or not help is wanted, is limited by the fact that rescuers who do too much for others without adequate compensation inevitably wind up feeling used and victimized by the people they have insisted on helping. Unless they can become conscious of what they are doing, rescuers get angry and eventually victimize the ones they are helping. Thus, in the attempt to recover what they have too freely given away, helpers easily become predators.

I see the rescue triangle as a shadow counterpart of the light Christian trinity. God the father, the Old Testament Yahweh, alternately rescued and persecuted His people, while Christ was both rescuing savior and sacrificial victim. When a person becomes identified with the Western God-image, he or she is likely to fall into one after another of these Godlike roles. At best, such a possession takes the form of a mild psychological co-dependence. In the worst case I have seen it manifest as a megalomania of psychotic proportions.

As far as I know, the only way out of possession by the raw power of the living God is to suffer it consciously, trying not to permit this part of the psyche to run amok, but examining it and doing everything possible to discover and honor its legitimate needs. This requires the development of a mature capacity for self-assertion that is willing to be responsible for the consequences of its actions, in sharp contrast to the emotionally-charged, childish and irresponsible demandingness typical of a person who is identified with a not-yet-transformed God-image.

Jung makes it clear that not everyone is up to the process of transforming the God within:

> . . . the divine incarnation . . . only manifests empirically in those relatively few individuals capable of enough consciousness to make ethical decisions, i.e., to decide for the Good. Therefore

God can be called good only inasmuch as He is able to manifest His goodness in individuals. His moral quality depends upon individuals. That is why He incarnates. Individuation and individual existence are indispensable for the transformation of God the Creator.[8]

In discussing this paragraph and the next, Edinger takes up the idea of psychological ethics, which, he says, does not just mean obeying the law or staying within the conventional social code, or even simply following one's conscience, for conscience is a mixture of internalized sanctions from other people who do not always know what is right for us, authentic directions from the Self, and psychological complexes that distort and confuse the issue. To begin to "decide for the Good" you have to get acquainted with the shadow in yourself and in others. "You can never be too sure where the good resides. It is not necessarily what looks best."

The apparent relativity of psychological ethics is not a sanction to break either the law or the conventional social code lightly. Such actions have consequences that cannot ethically be avoided.

In wrestling with ethical issues, I have found it useful to remind myself that nothing I do is all good. Everything has a dark side. Deciding for the good includes suffering the guilt for the harm that I cannot help doing no matter how good I try to be. However, the fact that it is impossible to live a blameless life does *not* mean that evil is good. The key to the problem of the shadow lies in bearing the guilt for it consciously instead of imagining that guilt can be avoided.

Jung gives the example that "generosity is certainly a virtue, but it instantly becomes a vice when applied to an individual that misunderstands it." When an act that appears to be generous is driven by uncon-

---

[8] See footnote 2.

scious power motives, it is sure to have bad effects. For instance, the parent who rescues a grown daughter from financial difficulty may keep her in a bond of eternal dependence by giving her the message that she is not competent to take care of herself. If, as is only human, the daughter continues to ask for financial help, the parent may feel victimized and retaliate by subtly or not so subtly abusing her. Thus does the rescue triangle spin on, fueled by the hidden shadow of a generous impulse.

In paragraph 6 of his letter to Elined Kotschnig, Jung expresses his admiration for the pious people of the Old Testament who dealt with Yahweh's dark side by asserting and invoking God's justice in the face of His obvious injustice. However, he says, those of us who were brought up to believe in a good God cannot stomach the inconsistency. "We cannot love and fear at the same time any more. Our consciousness has become too differentiated for such contradictions."

Here my experience differs from Jung's. I meet many women who were afraid of their fathers as children and now, as adults, have chosen husbands whom they love *and* fear even when they know it makes no sense. This is the dilemma of the individual who, once abused by a parent, is drawn as if by a magnet into the same kind of relationship, over and over again. The dynamic of the adult relationship can change dramatically when the woman becomes aware of her own participation in the drama of abuse and learns to carry her conflicting emotions consciously.

Just as bearing an insoluble personal conflict consciously can transform an individual, so can sufficient awareness of the contradictions in the Godhead change the God-image in the collective psyche. Jung continues:

We are . . . forced to take the fact of incarnation far more seriously than hitherto. We ought to remember that the Fathers of the Church have insisted upon the fact that God has given Himself to man's death on the Cross so that we may become gods.

I believe this is a hint that we are nearing a time when the general level of consciousness will no longer be able to tolerate wholesale denial of the extent of human power, particularly destructive power. In the 1940s, the development and use of the capacity to wage nuclear war caused a shock to the Western psyche that, for all practical purposes, destroyed our collective innocence. As we near the end of the millennium the nuclear danger has become negligible, but it may have served as an early warning of the host of other, perhaps worse threats that our Godalmightiness has contrived, putting our bodies, psyches and the earth itself at risk. It is now nearly impossible to go on pretending that control over life and death belongs to God alone. The divine opposites have come down from the heavens and into the human psyche where we have no choice but to come to terms with them. Jung goes on:

> The Deity has taken its abode in man with the obvious intention of realizing Its Good in man. Thus we are the vessel of the children and the heirs of the Deity suffering in the body of the "slave."

The "slave" refers to Philippians 2:6 where St. Paul says, "In your minds you must be the same as Christ Jesus: His state was divine, yet he did not cling to his equality with God but emptied himself *to assume the condition of a slave*, and became as men are." [Emphasis mine.] The church took up this idea as the doctrine of kenosis, which states that God had to empty himself of divinity to become human. Psychologically, it suggests that if we are to be vessels for the transformation of divine energy, our Godalmightiness must agree to enter consciousness and be limited.

This is similar to the idea Jung expressed elsewhere[9] that the spirit can go anywhere, but it only affects reality if it puts itself into a human

---

[9] *Nietzsche's Zarathustra*, vol 2 (Princeton: Princeton University Press, 1988), p. 815.

vessel, a specific body and psyche. In other words, to have real power in the real world, we have to leave the imaginal realm where we can do anything we wish, and submit to the painful truth of actual limitations.

The long final paragraph of Jung's letter to Elined Kotschnig begins with an excursion into the difference between Eastern and Western God-images. The subject was of some concern to him. Even though he admired Eastern thought and drew heavily upon it, he felt that grafting Eastern spiritual practices wholesale onto Western psyches did not work. Here he points out that the Eastern view expresses an important aspect of God, that of "eternal immovability," but that the God in whose image the Western psyche was made is in a dynamic process of development. Jung elaborated the historical development of the God-image in detail in *Answer to Job* and *Aion*, as described in the previous chapter. In the present context he summarizes:

> Its history begins with the plurality of the Elohim, then it comes to the paradoxical Oneness and personality of Yahweh, then to the good Father of Christianity, followed by the second Person in the Trinity, Christ, i.e., God incarnated in man. The . . . Holy Ghost is a third form . . . and finally we are confronted with the aspect revealed through the manifestations of the unconscious.

We all know people in whom we can observe each of the first steps: the lack of connection between who a person is from one hour or day to the next that is typical of plurality; the inconsistency and self-contradiction, now good and now bad character of paradoxical unity; the good Father; and Christlikeness. If we look carefully, we might even be able to see these parts of the God-image in our own behavior. The last two stages, the Holy Ghost, and the aspects of God revealed through the unconscious, are more internal. In my experience, the evolving individual tends to move through the stages in a sort of psychological equivalent of the biological principle that ontogeny recapitulates phylogeny, *i.e.*, the development of the individual repeats the steps involved in the evolution of the species. However, at least in the psychological realm, the previous stages do not entirely disappear.

The last stage, God as He manifests through the unconscious, represents a relatively new possibility in the psychological evolution of the species, one that not many people are able yet to reach. In the individual, it requires becoming aware of the various forms of Godlikeness in the psyche and answering for the worst, while aiming for the best, a development that gives an entirely new significance to human consciousness. As Jung puts it in the stunning conclusion to his letter:

> We have become participants of the divine life and we have to assume a new responsibility, viz. the continuation of the divine self-realization, which expresses itself in the task of our individuation. Individuation does not only mean that man has become truly human as distinct from animal, but that he is to become partially divine as well. This means practically that he becomes adult, responsible for his existence, knowing that he does not only depend on God but that God also depends on man. Man's relation to God probably has to undergo a certain important change: Instead of the propitiating praise to an unpredictable king or the child's prayer to a loving father, the responsible living and fulfilling of the divine will in us will be our form of worship of and commerce with God. His goodness means grace and light and His dark side the terrible temptation of power. Man has already received so much knowledge that he can destroy his own planet. Let us hope that God's good spirit will guide him

in his decisions, because it will depend upon man's decision whether God's creation will continue. Nothing shows more drastically than this possibility how much of divine power has come within the reach of man.

Writing about these matters is a risky business. It heats up the archetype and sets it in motion like the molecules in a pot of boiling water. Before you know it, the thing you are talking about spills into your life.

As soon as I begin to consider "the responsible living and fulfilling of the divine will," sickness strikes. Nothing life-threatening. Not even an honest flu, but one of those insidious, tenacious, mononucleosis-like viruses that nibble away at a person's energy until, suddenly, nothing is left.

I had the following dream:

I open my wallet to pay for some pie I have ordered at a restaurant and discover that my money is gone. I know I had a $100 bill, and a $50 and some $20s. I keep looking through the papers I keep in my wallet, but the money is definitely gone. Someone has stolen it and arranged the papers to conceal the theft. I can hardly believe it. I think, "Well, I can pay with a credit card," because my credit-card holder seems to be in order. But when I look more closely, I see that the credit cards have also been taken and the other items carefully put back to disguise the loss.

If a patient reported this dream, and was as overextended in her life as I was in mine, I might say, "You probably don't feel it yet, but your reserves are depleted. There is nothing left, not even a little credit. If you drop everything *right now* and go to bed for a few days, you might be able to renew your resources. Otherwise, don't be surprised if you get sick."

Do I apply my good advice to myself? Of course not. The contractor is breathing down my neck because I have not yet decided on carpet, tile, or the location of electrical outlets for the house David and I are building; David is in bed with flu; we have just run out of toilet paper, and besides, I have to explain what "the responsible living and fulfilling of the divine will" means, and also "the terrible temptation of power." So here I am in the grip of a blind, driven thing and cannot stop trying to power my way through.

After I have been sick for several weeks, the AIDS fantasies begin. I feel as if my brain has turned to mush, and it is easy to believe that I became infected during my promiscuous 40s in Los Angeles. I imagine that a vengeful God has sent me HIV for not fulfilling His will, that I have passed it on to the man I love, and that neither of us will survive long enough to live in the new house.

"Write! Write!" screams the blind creator within me. "Don't stop now. Time is running out."

"Wait," I say. "God doesn't want me to go on with this project. If He did, He wouldn't make it so hard. If I am going to fulfill the divine will in me, I have to back out of my commitment to speak to the Quakers."

"That's the wrong answer," snaps the blind creator. "Write!"

"Maybe I'm like Job," I think. "Maybe I'm not doing anything wrong at all. Maybe Satan, God's left-hand man, has tempted Him to strike down a completely virtuous woman."

About then, the fever begins. "All right," I say, "I'll go to bed for a day. *Two* days even. I'll give you the whole weekend to fix me. By Monday, I want this thing cleared up. . . . Please," I add, not wanting to presume too much upon God's good will.

The weekend in bed provides a welcome opportunity to read the birthday present David gave me, a biography of Woody Allen with whom I feel a secret kinship. I learn that Woody finished writing one of his scripts while in bed with a high fever and incipient pneumonia. Apparently he and I are less alike than I want to believe.

Woody is reputed to be a hypochondriac who takes his temperature every two hours. By Sunday afternoon, I am putting the thermometer in my mouth once an hour or more. The reading hangs steady at 101.2.

"God, what are you doing" I say? "Are you trying to make a complete fool of me? Do you want me to give half a lecture and then stand there and say, 'Well folks, that's all. Sorry. I've done my best and I just can't go on.'"

Suddenly the clenched fist in the middle of my chest lets go and I think, "Well, would that be so bad? I have my limits. I'm only human."

Then I say to the blind creator, "OK. You win. I'll stay in bed tomorrow, and the next day, and the day after that. However long it takes." When I take my temperature again it has dropped to normal. By morning I have a little energy, and a day or two later, slowly, slowly, I begin to write again.

So it is not so simple to discover what the divine will in us wants, let alone to do it. Edinger even suggests—and I think he is right—that God may not know what His will is until *we* discover it. He may be dependent on us to make Him aware of what He wants.

In view of the shocking things Jung says about God's destructiveness, how can he define maturity as "the responsible living and fulfilling of the divine will in us"? I believe the operative word is "responsible." We cannot merely do what God wants, even when we think we know what it is, because the blind, untransformed God is dangerously irresponsible. Only through human consciousness does responsibility come into the equation. The transpersonal center inside that feels like the will of God—the thing that, as Edinger puts it, is calling the shots—is concerned with our unique, individual destiny and cares not a fig about our fellow human beings. To fulfill the divine will in a way that is not too destructive we have to wrestle with conflicting obligations. But God help us if we forget where the power resides. It is a terrible temptation to claim divine power for the glory of the ego. If you lose touch with the fact that the ego must ultimately serve the Self, not the other way around, the fire of the living God can burn you alive. It is the sort of mistake that can put you in bed with a fever.

• • •

In the Gospel according to Matthew we read: "And Jesus, when he was baptized, went up straightway out of the water: and, lo, the heavens were opened unto him, and he saw the Spirit of God descending like a dove, and lighting upon him. And lo a voice from heaven, saying, This is my beloved son in whom I am well pleased."[10]

What an experience of grace and light this must have been for Jesus, truly a manifestation of God's goodness! However, Edinger points out that in the very next sentence "Jesus was led up of the spirit into the wilderness to be tempted of the devil."[11] Apparently the two things go together. When the Self—the God-image in the psyche—is activated, it brings both grace and light and the temptations of power.

Jesus solved the problem of power by separating himself decisively from it: "Get thee hence, Satan!" Jung, in his letter to Kotschnig, hints that we no longer have this option, for "[We have] already received so much knowledge that [we] can destroy [our] own planet. Let us hope that God's good spirit will guide [us] in [our] decisions, because it will depend upon [our] decision whether God's creation will continue." We have to open our eyes and look at the power in our hands and take responsibility for what we do with it. This is quite different from, even antithetical to, the Christian ideal of meekness and humility, but as we have seen, the Christian ideal casts a black shadow. Denying power or saying we do not

---

[10] Matthew 3:16–17.
[11] Matthew 4:1.

want it only insures that it will come out in ways that unconsciousness makes all the more destructive, like the roles of the rescue triangle.

Just what *is* the "terrible temptation of power"? The question has many answers, a number of which seem to me to fall into the category of overstepping boundaries, either violating the rights of others or going beyond human limitations. Wrestling with the temptations of power teaches us where our own and others' limits are. In the process we learn not to presume too much upon others and also how important it is to protect our own boundaries. When we permit another person to trespass on our space, we share the guilt of his presumption.

So it is that living and fulfilling the divine will requires the most exquisite consciousness of power, something of which the Christian era has taught us little. As I see it, the process of individuation entails the gradual discovery, through trial and error, of exactly how much and what kind of power rightfully belongs to a particular individual, in the course of which the unconscious God-image inside becomes conscious and is tempered until it can be lived in a mature and responsible way.

chapter seven

AND LAST

The dynamic of this process [of individuation] is instinct, which ensures that everything which belongs to an individual's life shall enter into it, whether he consents or not, or is conscious of what is happening to him or not.
—C. G. JUNG[1]

At the beginning of the Biblical Book of Job, Satan tempts Yahweh to believe that the innocent man Job is not as virtuous as he seems to be, and that, under duress, Job would not remain loyal to Him. Cast into doubt, God hunts Job down and puts him to the test. By the tenth chapter, Yahweh has inflicted so much harm upon Job, his family, and his possessions that the wronged man gives vent to his anguish, no longer caring whether he lives or dies. In the midst of his lengthy complaint, Job says to God:

> Woe to me, if I am guilty; if I am innocent, I dare not lift my head, so wholly abject, so drunk with pain am I./ And if I make

---

[1] CW 11, ¶745.

a stand, like a lion you hunt me down, adding to the tale of your triumphs./ You attack, and attack me again, with stroke on stroke of your fury, relentlessly your fresh troops assail me.[2]

The image of God as a savage hunter or bloodthirsty animal whose prey is humankind crops up in a number of contexts. In *Thus Spake Zarathustra* Nietzsche writes:

> Stretched out, shuddering,/ Like a half-dead thing whose feet are warmed,/ Shaken by unknown fevers,/ Shivering with piercing icy frost arrows,/ Hunted by thee, O thought,/ Unutterable! Veiled! horrible one!/ Thou huntsman behind the clouds. Struck down by thy lightning bolt,/ Thou mocking eye that stares at me from the dark! Thus I lie,/ Writhing, twisting, tormented/ With all eternal tortures,/ Smitten/ By thee, cruel huntsman,/ Thou unknown—God![3]

The idea that God is as much killer as savior is also discernible in some contemporary works of art and literature. For instance, the 1978 movie "The Deer Hunter" has as a central image the game of Russian roulette, which embodies the perception that God, or fate, hunts a man down and kills or spares him utterly unpredictably. The theme is echoed in the film's protagonist Michael, who appears to be something of a God-image. Initially Michael presents a very primitive picture, a steelworker who takes great pride in his ability to kill a deer with a single shot. Then he and two friends are sent to Viet Nam, where they are captured by the enemy and subjected to experiences at the far edge of human endurance. The friends

---

[2] Job 10:15–17.
[3] Friedrich Wilhelm Nietzsche, "Thus Spoke Zarathustra," in The Portable Nietzsche (New York: Viking, 1954), LXV—"The Magician."

go mad, each in his own way, but Michael's suffering raises him to a Christlike level of compassion. When, after his return home, he goes deer-hunting again, his predatory prowess is sacrificed. The film does not make clear whether Michael decides consciously not to kill another deer or simply finds that he cannot shoot, but in either case, his killer instincts are transformed.

The ambiguity about *why* Michael does not shoot the deer brings to mind the question sometimes asked about Jesus: Did he choose His fate as carrier of the divine sacrifice or was it imposed upon him? Looking at the crucifixion as it manifests internally, as a process in the psyche, I have to conclude that the answer is not one or the other but both. That is, the God within can only be transformed when the Self demands it *and* the ego assents. If either partner fails to participate fully the process is likely to go wrong, as exemplified by Michael's two friends.

Rivkah Kluger provides still another allusion to the motif of God as predator when she says that the Israelites became Yahweh's chosen people because they were, in a manner of speaking, "God's easiest prey."[4] This reveals how dubious an honor it is to be chosen, and suggests that being elected to take part in the transformation of the God-image in the collective psyche is in some ways the same as being killed. This death is symbolic, however, in contrast to the premature literal death sometimes suffered by people who cannot respond to the call to individuate. As Jung puts it, each of us is an experiment of the Self, and if the experiment fails, we die.[5] I have seen this happen tragically on more than one occasion.

It is as if the divine impulse seeking to enter a particular human life *will* have it, if not in one way, then in another. A person who becomes a

---

[4] Rivkah S. Kluger, *Psyche and Bible* (Zurich: Spring Publications, 1974), p. 41.

[5] I regret that I cannot cite the source of this remark, which I read many years ago. I believe it comes from the unpublished notes for one of Jung's seminars, but have not been able to locate it.

target of the divine will cannot avoid being shot down, but if she is conscious enough and young enough she may be able to choose a symbolic death rather than a literal one.

When a person says yes to the call of the Self, the ensuing symbolic death grows out of the painful realization that something beyond the ego, with different intentions and goals, is trying to lead the way. The necessary sacrifice of the ego's demand for supremacy is like a death on the cross.

• • •

Autumn has come and David and I are taking our annual hike on the Spruce Railroad Trail along Lake Crescent's bluffy shoreline. My attention is caught by two birds that appear to be engaged in some sort of dance, fifty yards or so out over the water. Although they are nearly the same size one of them, a hawk, is pursuing the other. We cannot make out the identity of the prey-bird. Its attempts to elude the predator are awkward and the distance between the birds is closing. Suddenly the prey-bird plummets toward the lake. When it hits the water there is a sharp report, like the sound of a person doing a belly-flop. The hawk circles hopefully for a moment, then flies away.

The prey-bird is swimming toward the shore. Its movements are clumsy and it appears to be getting waterlogged. This is no duck. We are not at all certain that it will be able to reach land.

It struggles on, however, and we walk back along the trail to intersect its trajectory. Standing at a respectful distance, we watch it drag itself out of the water and, in a last desperate lunge, heave itself onto a large rock where it lies splayed in exhaustion. We are astonished to see that it is a grouse, a female. I fear that she will not survive, but David believes she will rest until the sun has dried her feathers and then go about her grouse business. We continue hiking to the end of the trail and come back by the same route. When we return, the rock is empty and the grouse has vanished into the woods.

Peterson's *Field Guide to Western Birds* describes grouse as "ground-dwelling, chicken-like birds." There is no mention of any ability to swim. Apparently, under exceptional circumstances, even a so-called lower animal can act *contra naturam* and go beyond the limitations of her species to evade a horrible early death.

• • •

Not long after becoming interested in Jung's work I went to a lecture by Joe Wheelwright, one of the first Jungian analysts in San Francisco. I have forgotten much of what he said, but one sentence struck me like lightning:

"The reason I became a Jungian is because I don't want to die screaming."

I did not understand exactly what he meant, but I knew it was important and have thought about it many times in the nearly forty years since.

For as long as I can remember I have watched old people and made mental notes as if I were preparing for a test, and of course, in a way, that is what I have been doing. As a child I eavesdropped endlessly on my elders' obsessions, wrinkling my nose at Grandad's fulminations about his bowels and Aunt Gertrude's on the subject of her liver, lungs, and other bodily functions. I vowed to remember, and promised myself that I would *never* indulge in such disgusting behavior. And of course I do remember, and am forced to break my promise daily.

Later, when I was a young analyst, I watched my aging colleagues for clues about what might happen to me in the decades to come. In time I realized that losing control of the body is not the half of it. For many, giving up power over others is a far worse ordeal. I noticed that some people cling to their authority so tenaciously that, when they can no longer carry it, it has to be wrested from them. Some, on the other hand, pass the baton gracefully as soon as the time is right.

I have wondered what makes the difference between people who give up their power easily and those who do not, and believe the key may lie in Jung's observation, quoted at the beginning of this chapter, that "everything which belongs to an individual's life shall enter into it."[6] My guess is that the people who assiduously take up the tasks of the Self as they come, fulfilling their inner development as best they can, will be ready to move on at each new stage of life, even the final one.

The experience of my friends and relatives, patients and colleagues confirms that everything suppressed, repressed, denied, or simply unseen in a person will eventually come out. I feel it would be futile to turn away from anything that knocks on my inner door, no matter how loathsome, for if I do not face it while I am young enough to integrate it consciously, it will be out there for everyone to see in my dotage. When courage fails and I am tempted to hide behind compliant and collectively acceptable behavior, I revisit the memory of my father's late-life madness, or recall a once gracious and charming neighbor, the very personification of Christian charity, who in her 80th year became hateful, vicious, and crude, as disagreeable a specimen of humanity as I ever expect to meet. Examples like these are all the reason I need to stay true to my individual path, for they demonstrate that everything that belongs to a person *does* come home, if not at the right time, then in predictably offensive ways as the body declines.

I believe that taking responsibility for everything that belongs to me, even for transforming the part of the godhead that dwells in me, contributes to making the world a better place to live. By carrying my portion of untransformed God-energy consciously, I believe that I remove it from the general supply, thereby reducing the collective pressure toward

---

[6] CW II, ¶745.

war, terrorism, mass murder, and other out-of-control forms of violence. Moreover, by accepting the unacceptable parts of myself while I am still conscious enough to integrate them, I believe I increase my chances for a more or less decent end.

To the extent that these beliefs are subjective articles of faith, they are part of my personal religious path. On the other hand, to the extent that they are objectively true they are science, for they come from careful observations of the psyche in its various manifestations, repeated many times and under many different conditions. Observations like these, that satisfy both the scientific and the religious sides of myself, are the only ways of looking at life that fully meet my needs.

• • •

I dream that it is evening, just as in outer reality it is the evening of my life.

> In the dream I am about to go for a walk, but at the corner of my property, just before crossing a little bridge, I stop cold. A mountain lion is standing on the other side of the bridge, a beautiful, sleek animal, larger than life and considerably taller than I. The creature stands and looks at me, then gathers itself as if to attack. I think, "It's all over." I remember reading, however, that if you meet a mountain lion, it may be possible to avoid being eaten by facing the animal and making yourself look as large as possible.

Looking large is not easy for me, for I am less than an inch taller than five feet, but I stand on tiptoe and raise my hands as high over my head as they will go. Then I begin to growl, a low, throaty growl. The animal hesitates, backs off, and finally, after a long, uncertain moment, turns tail and walks away.

JUNG'S LETTER TO ELINED KOTSCHNIG[1]

[*Mrs. Kotschnig had asked for an answer to the problem of an unconscious, ignorant creator god and if this did not imply "some principle, some Ground of Being, beyond such a demiurge."*]

30 JUNE 1956

Dear Mrs. Kotschnig,

It is not quite easy to answer your question within the space of a letter. You know that we human beings are unable to explain anything that happens without or within ourselves otherwise than through the use of the intellectual means at our disposal. We always have to use mental elements similar to the facts we believe we have observed. Thus when we try to explain how God has created His world or how He behaves toward the world, the analogy we use is the way in which our creative spirit produces and behaves. When we consider the data of paleontology with the view that a conscious

¶ I

¶1 creator has perhaps spent more than a thousand million years, and has made, as it seems to us, no end of detours to produce consciousness, we inevitably come to the conclusion that—if we want to explain His doing at all—His behavior is strikingly similar to a being with an at least very limited consciousness. Although aware of the things that are the next steps to take, He has apparently neither foresight of an ulterior goal nor any knowledge of a direct way to reach it. Thus it would not be an absolute unconsciousness but a rather dim consciousness. Such a consciousness would necessarily produce any amount of errors and impasses with the most cruel consequences, disease, mutilation, and horrible fights, i.e., just the thing that has happened and is still happening throughout all realms of life. Moreover it is impossible for us to assume that a Creator producing a universe out of nothingness can be conscious of anything, because each act of cognition is based upon a discrimination—for instance, I cannot be conscious of somebody else when I am identical with him. If there is nothing outside of God everything is God and in such a state there is simply no possibility of self-cognition.

¶2 Nobody can help admitting that the thought of a God creating any amount of errors and impasses is as good as a catastrophe. When the original Jewish conception of a purposeful and morally inclined God marked the end of the playful and rather purposeless existence of the polytheistic deities in the Mediterranean sphere, the result was a paradoxical conception of the supreme being, finding its expression in the idea of divine justice and injustice. The clear recognition of the fatal unreliability of the deity led Jewish prophecy to look for a sort of mediator or advocate, representing the claims of humanity before God. As you know, this figure is already announced in Ezekiel's vision of the

Man and Son of Man.[2] The idea was carried on by Daniel[3] and then in the Apocryphal writings, particularly in the figure of the female Demiurge, viz. Sophia,[4] and in the male form of an administrator of justice, the Son of Man, in the Book of Enoch, written about 100 B.C. and very popular at the time of Christ. It must have been so well-known, indeed, that Christ called himself "Son of Man" with the evident presupposition of everybody knowing what he was talking about. Enoch is exactly what the Book of Job expects the advocate of man to be, over against the lawlessness and moral unreliability of Yahweh. The recently discovered scrolls of the Dead Sea mention a sort of legendary figure, viz. "the Teacher of Justice."[5] I think he is parallel to or identical with Enoch. Christ obviously took up this idea, feeling that his task was to represent the role of the "Teacher of Justice" and thus of a Mediator, and he was up against an unpredictable and lawless God who would need a most drastic sacrifice to appease His wrath, viz. the slaughter of His own son. Curiously enough, as on the one hand his self-sacrifice means admission of the Father's amoral nature, he taught on the other hand a new image of God, namely that of a Loving Father in whom there is no darkness. This enormous antinomy needs some explanation. It needed the assertion that he was the Son of the Father, i.e., the incarnation of the Deity in man. As a consequence the sacrifice was a self-destruction of the amoral God, incarnated in a mortal body. Thus

¶2

---

[2] Ezekiel 1:16ff.

[3] Daniel 7:13ff.

[4] Proverbs 8:22ff.

[5] The Teacher of Justice, or of Righteousness, was the name given to the leader of a Jewish sect (probably the Essenes), parts of whose literature, the Dead Sea Scrolls, were found in 1947 (and after) near Qumran, northwest of the Dead Sea. The Essenes were an ascetic sect founded in the 2nd cent. B.C., living in communities in the Judaean desert.

¶2 the sacrifice takes on the aspect of a highly moral deed, of a self-punishment, as it were.

¶3 Inasmuch as Christ is understood to be the second Person of the Trinity, the self-sacrifice is the evidence for God's goodness. At least so far as human beings are concerned. We don't know whether there are other inhabited worlds where the same divine evolution has taken place. It is thinkable that there are many inhabited worlds in different stages of development where God has not yet undergone the transformation through incarnation. However that may be, for us earthly beings the incarnation has taken place and we have become participants in the divine nature and presumably heirs of the tendency towards goodness and at the same time subject to the inevitable self-punishment. As Job was not a mere spectator of divine unconsciousness but fell a victim to this momentous manifestation, in the case of incarnation we also become involved in the consequences of this transformation. Inasmuch as God proves His goodness through self-sacrifice He is incarnated, but in view of His infinity and the presumably different stages of cosmic development we don't know of, how much of God—if this is not too human an argument—has been transformed? In this case it can be expected that we are going to contact spheres of a not-yet-transformed God when our consciousness begins to extend into the sphere of the unconscious. There is at all events a definite expectation of the kind expressed in the "Evangelium Aeternum" of the Revelation containing the message: Fear God![6]

¶4 Although the divine incarnation is a cosmic and absolute event, it only manifests empirically in those relatively few individuals capable of enough consciousness to make ethical decisions, i.e., to

---

[6] Rev. 14:6–7.

decide for the Good. Therefore God can be called good only inasmuch as He is able to manifest His goodness in individuals. His moral quality depends upon individuals. That is why He incarnates. Individuation and individual existence are indispensable for the transformation of God the Creator.

¶4

The knowledge of what is good is not given *a priori*; it needs discriminating consciousness. That is already the problem in Genesis, where Adam and Eve have to be enlightened first in order to recognize the Good and discriminate it from Evil. There is no such thing as the "Good" in general, because something that is definitely good can be as definitely evil in another case. Individuals are different from each other, their values are different and their situations vary to such an extent that they cannot be judged by general values and principles. For instance generosity is certainly a virtue, but it instantly becomes a vice when applied to an individual that misunderstands it. In this case one needs conscious discrimination.

¶5

Your question concerning the relationship between the human being and an unconscious paradoxical God is indeed a major question, although we have the most impressive paradigm of Old Testament piety that could deal with the divine antinomy. The people of the Old Testament could address themselves to an unreliable God. By very overt attempts at propitiation I mean in particular the repeated assertion and invocation of god's justice and this in the face of indisputable injustice. They tried to avoid His wrath and to call forth His goodness. It is quite obvious that the old Hebrew theologians were continuously tormented by the fear of Yahweh's unpredictable acts of injustice.

¶6

For the Christian mentality, brought up in the conviction of an essentially good God, the situation is much more difficult. One cannot love and fear at the same time any more. Our consciousness has

¶7

¶7

become too differentiated for such contradictions. We are therefore forced to take the fact of incarnation far more seriously than hitherto. We ought to remember that the Fathers of the Church have insisted upon the fact that God has given Himself to man's death on the Cross so that we may become gods. The Deity has taken its abode in man with the obvious intention of realizing Its Good in man. Thus we are the vessel of the children and the heirs of the Deity suffering in the body of the "slave."[7]

¶8

We are now in a position to understand the essential point of view of our brethren the Hindus. They are aware of the fact that the personal Atman is identical with the universal Atman and have evolved ways and means to express the psychological consequences of such a belief. In this respect we have to learn something from them. It saves us from spiritual pride when we humbly recognize that God can manifest Himself in many different ways. Christianity has envisaged the religious problem as a sequence of dramatic events, whereas the East holds a thoroughly static view, i.e., a cyclic view. The thought of evolution is Christian and—as I think—in a way a better truth to express the dynamic aspect of the Deity, although the eternal immovability also forms an important aspect of the Deity (in Aristotle and in the old scholastic philosophy). The religious spirit of the West is characterized by a change of God's image in the course of ages. Its history begins with the plurality of the Elohim, then it comes to the paradoxical Oneness and personality of Yahweh, then to the good Father of Christianity, followed by the second Person in the Trinity, Christ, i.e., God incarnated in man. The allusion to the Holy Ghost is a third form appearing at

---

[7] Or "servant." Cf. Phil. 2:6.

the beginning of the Christian age (Gioacchino da Fiore),[8] and finally we are confronted with the aspect revealed through the manifestations of the unconscious. The significance of man is enhanced by the incarnation. We have become participants of the divine life and we have to assume a new responsibility, viz. the continuation of the divine self-realization, which expresses itself in the task of our individuation. Individuation does not only mean that man has become truly human as distinct from animal, but that he is to become partially divine as well. This means practically that he becomes adult, responsible for his existence, knowing that he does not only depend on God but that God also depends on man. Man's relation to God probably has to undergo a certain important change: Instead of the propitiating praise to an unpredictable king or the child's prayer to a loving father, the responsible living and fulfilling of the divine will in us will be our form of worship of and commerce with God. His goodness means grace and light and His dark side the terrible temptation of power. Man has already received so much knowledge that he can destroy his own planet. Let us hope that God's good spirit will guide him in his decisions, because it will depend upon man's decision whether God's creation will continue. Nothing shows more drastically than this possibility how much of divine power has come within the reach of man.

If anything of the above should not be clear to you, I am quite ready for further explanation.

Sincerely yours,

C. G. Jung

---

[8] Cf. White, 24 Nov. 53, n. 10. [The 12th-century Italian mystic Joachim of Flora taught that there are three periods of world history: the Age of the Law, or the Father; the Age of the Gospel, or the Son; and the Age of the Holy Spirit, or Contemplation.] Brackets mine.

BIBLIOGRAPHY

Burland, C. A. *The Arts of the Alchemists*. New York: Macmillan, 1968.

Dallett, Janet O. *Saturday's Child: Encounters with the Dark Gods*. Toronto: Inner City Books, 1991.

————. *When the Spirits Come Back*. Toronto: Inner City Books, 1988.

DeLillo, Don. *Underworld*. New York: Scribner, 1997.

de Vries, Ad. *Dictionary of Symbols and Imagery*. Amsterdam: Elsevier, 1974.

Dinnage, Rosemary. "The Whirr of Wings" (review of *Virginia Woolf*, by Hermione Lee), *The New York Review of Books*, May 29, 1997, pp. 4–6.

Edinger, Edward F. *Anatomy of the Psyche*. La Salle, IL: Open Court, 1985.

————. *The Bible and the Psyche*. Toronto: Inner City Books, 1986.

————. *Ego and Archetype*. Baltimore: Penguin Books, 1973.

————. *The New God-Image: A Study of Jung's Key Letters Concerning the Evolution of the Western God-Image*, Dianne D. Cordic and Charles Yates, eds. Wilmette, IL: Chiron Publications, 1996.

————. *Transformation of the God-Image*. Toronto: Inner City Books, 1992.

————. "The New God-Image." Seminar at the C. G. Jung Institute, Los Angeles, 1991–1992. 10 audio tapes.

Eliade, Mircea. *Shamanism.* Princeton: Princeton University Press, 1964.

Holy Bible. King James Version.

Jaffé, Aniela. *From the Life and Work of C. G. Jung,* R. F. C. Hull, trans. New York: Harper & Row, 1971.

Jung, C. G. *C. G. Jung Speaking,* William McGuire and R. F. C. Hull, eds. Princeton: Princeton University Press, 1977.

———. *Collected Works of C. G. Jung* (Bollingen Series XX), R. F. C. Hull, trans. H. Read, M. Fordham, G. Adler, W. McGuire, eds. Princeton: Princeton University Press, 1953–1979. 20 volumes.

Vol. 4, *Freud and Psychoanalysis,* 1961.

Vol. 8, *The Structure and Dynamics of the Psyche,* 1960.

Vol. 9–II, *Aion,* 1959.

Vol. 10, *Civilization in Transition,* 1964.

Vol. 11, *Psychology and Religion,* 1958.

Vol. 12, *Psychology and Alchemy,* 1953.

Vol. 13, *Alchemical Studies,* 1967.

Vol. 14, *Mysterium Coniunctionis,* 1963.

Vol. 15, *The Spirit in Man, Art, and Literature,* 1966.

Vol. 16, *The Practice of Psychotherapy,* 1954.

Vol. 18, *The Symbolic Life,* 1976.

———. *Letters* (Bollingen Series XCV). R. F. C. Hull, trans. Gerhard Adler and Aniela Jaffé, eds. Princeton: Princeton University Press, 1973. 2 volumes.

———. *Memories, Dreams, Reflections.* Aniela Jaffé, ed. New York: Pantheon, 1961.

———. *Nietzsche's Zarathustra,* seminar notes. James L. Jarrett, ed. Princeton: Princeton University Press, 1988. 2 volumes.

———. *The Visions Seminars.* Zurich: Spring Publications, 1976.

———. "Letters to Oskar Schmitz, 1921–1931," *Psychological Perspectives,* 2 volumes. Zurich: Spring Publications, 1975.

Karpman, Stephen. "Fairy Tales and Script Drama Analysis," *Transactional Analysis Bulletin*, 7:39–43, April, 1968.

Kluger, Rivkah S. *Psyche and Bible*. Zurich: Spring Publications, 1974.

Moyers, Bill. *Joseph Campbell and the Power of Myth*. New York: Mystic Fire Video, 1988. 6 video tapes.

Nietzsche, Friedrich Wilhelm. "Thus Spoke Zarathustra," in *The Portable Nietzsche*, Walter Kaufmann, trans. New York: Viking Press, 1954.

Potok, Chaim. *The Book of Lights*. New York: Alfred A. Knopf, 1981.

Steiner, Claude. "The Rescue Triangle," photocopied paper, privately circulated.

Van der Post, Laurens. *Jung & the Story of Our Time*. New York: Pantheon Books, 1975.

Zeller, Max. *The Dream: The Vision of the Night*. Janet Dallett, ed. Boston: Sigo Press, 1990.

INDEX

David Mathieson

Janet O. Dallett is a Jungian analyst and a freelance writer. She has published articles and reviews in the *Whole Earth Review, Psychological Perspectives, Psychological Bulletin, Quadrant, Voices: The Art and Science of Psychotherapy, The San Francisco Jung Institute Library Journal*. She received a B.A. in psychology from Kalamazoo College in Michigan, her Ph.D. in psychology from UCLA, and her training as a Jungian analyst at the C. G. Jung Institute, Los Angeles. She was the Director of Training at the Jung Institute in Los Angeles from 1976–1978, taught there from 1974–1983, and also practiced during this time. She moved to Port Townsend, WA in 1983, where she still has a practice, and devotes time to writing. She is the author of two books: *When the Spirits Come Back* and *Saturday's Child: Encounters with the Dark Gods*, both published by Inner City Books in Toronto.